D1454601

COMHAIRLE CHONTAE ÁTHA CLIATH THEAS
SOUTH DUBLIN COUNTY LIBRARIES

SOUTH DUBLIN BOOKSTORE
TO RENEW ANY ITEM TEL: 459 7834

Items should be returned on or before the last date below. Fines,
as displayed in the Library, will be charged on overdue items.

PIMPERNEL GOLD

Pimpernel Gold

HOW NORWAY FOILED THE NAZIS

DOROTHY BADEN-POWELL

FOREWORD BY
Sir Laurence Collier, K.C.M.G.

ST. MARTIN'S PRESS
NEW YORK

ROBERT HALE LIMITED
LONDON

© Dorothy Baden-Powell 1978
First published 1978

St. Martin's Press, Inc.
175 Fifth Avenue
New York, N.Y. 10010

Library of Congress Catalog Card Number: 77–14680

Library of Congress Cataloging in Publication Data

Baden-Powell, Dorothy.
  Pimpernel gold.

  1. World War, 1939–1945—Underground movements—
Norway. 2. Norway—History—German occupation,
1940–1945. I. Title.
D802.N7B3   940.53′481   77–14680
  ISBN 0-312-61165-x

Robert Hale Limited
Clerkenwell House
Clerkenwell Green
London EC1R 0HT

ISBN 0 7091 6748 2

Printed in Great Britain by
Clarke, Doble & Brendon Ltd,
Plymouth and London

CONTENTS

ILLUSTRATIONS

MAPS

FOREWORD

By Sir Laurence Collier, K.C.M.G.

British Representative to the Royal Norwegian Government in London, 1941–45, and afterwards British Ambassador to Norway

I HAVE READ and enjoyed the manuscript of this book. Though it reads like a first-class 'thriller', I can testify that it is a record of historical fact. The author, bilingual and half-Norwegian, worked during the war in the Norwegian section of S.O.E., and is known to me. So was her cousin, Colonel Ole-Jacob Broch, who held the post of General Krigskommissaer (Quartermaster-General) in the Norwegian High Command in London during the war.

I think it is high time that this dramatic story, the first of a number of exploits by the Norwegian Resistance, should be given the publicity it deserves in this country.

LAURENCE COLLIER

FOR RUTH MONTEFIORE

PREFACE

DURING THE Second World War I was privileged to work with
the men organizing resistance in Norway.

The first assignment in which members of my own particular groups were involved was the rescue of the Norwegian
gold reserves in 1940. In the words of Mr Carl J. Hambro,
President of the Norwegian Storting in 1940: "Care had to be
taken of the gold of the Bank of Norway, the reserves so
vitally important to the future of the Kingdom of Norway.
Loaded on trucks, drawn on sledges where the condition of
the road was bad, unguarded but protected by the instincts
of a whole nation, the gold came all the way through the
Gudbrandsdal and across to the fjords. How it was taken out
of Oslo, how all those many tons of bullion worth more than
a hundred million dollars, were carried along with the Army,
in front of the Army, is a fantastic modern romance."

It occurred to me that it would add to an already exciting
story if I could find out what action, if any, the enemy were
taking to capture the bullion, and whether the Germans
encountered by those responsible for the gold were actually
looking for it, or looking for the King and the Government,
or merely trying to secure strong-points behind the lines.

During the course of my researches I have been given a
mass of relevant data in three languages from a variety of
official sources, and I am most grateful to all those who have
taken the trouble to help me. I refer principally to the
officials of the Royal Norwegian Embassy in London, the
Norwegian Ministry of Defence, the British Ministry of
Defence, the German Embassy in London and their War
History Department in West Germany, and the librarians of
the Imperial War Museum in London. And finally I was put
in touch with a German Army officer, Major Wolfgang
Lindauer, who served on the staff of General von Falkenhorst

during the invasion of Norway. He has been good enough to give me his version of events from his point of view in so far as they affected the journey of the gold bullion, and his information adds an entirely new dimension to the story.

DOROTHY BADEN-POWELL
Ballindoon House
Co. Roscommon
Eire

ONE

HITLER'S BLUNDER: VIDKUN QUISLING

GENERAL VON FALKENHORST, commanding officer of the German invading forces in Norway, was still sitting in temporary headquarters near to Dröbak. If the attack had gone according to plan, the whole town of Oslo should have been in German hands by now, and he and his staff settled in. Major Quisling, the man Hitler had chosen to become the puppet Norwegian Prime Minister, had assured the Führer that Norway would offer no resistance to the Germans when they landed—that, on the contrary, they would be greeted as friends. But, armed only with their rifles and some hand-grenades, the Norwegians were fighting back, and fighting hard. He had been obliged to report the situation to Berlin. The memorandum containing the German terms for the immediate surrender of Norway, accompanied by threats as to what would happen to them if they offered the slightest resistance to the German invasion, had been presented to the Norwegian Government by the German Minister at 0430 precisely, as scheduled, but at the time, owing to an unfortunate hold-up at Dröbak, Oslo was not in German hands; the memorandum had been rejected, and the Norwegian Government had decided to fight it out and take the consequences. It had been hoped that Quisling's pro-German propaganda would have been sufficiently effective for Norwegians to have refused to fight the Germans whatever their Government said; there was only one way to find out, and that was to have the memorandum, a copy of which was lying on his desk, published in the national newspapers. Then perhaps there would be an end to this nonsense.

Sitting beside him was Major Lindauer, the bearer of the unfortunate news that the German ships had been spotted by a coastguard at Filtvedt on their way up the Oslofjord, who had made a report to Naval Headquarters before they had been able to get through the Dröbak Narrows. From that

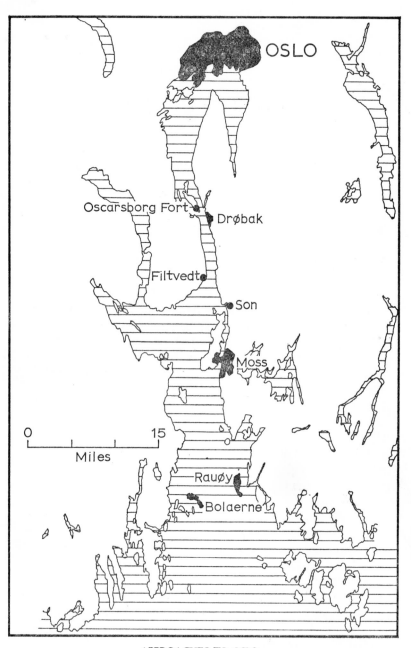

OSLO

Oscarsborg Fort
Drøbak

Filtvedt
Son

Moss

0   15
Miles

Rauøy
Bolaerne

APPROACHES TO OSLO

moment on, all hell had been let loose. The guns of coastal forts marked as 'obsolete' on the German charts had proved that they could still be used, and with accuracy, and a large number of German ships had been sunk by ancient and indifferently armed Norwegian vessels. The worst setback had been the sinking of the new cruiser *Blücher* by the guns of the Oscarsborg Fortress, which had appeared on the German charts as a 'museum'. She had been in the lead steaming up the Oslofjord; the ships following her, thinking she had struck a mine, turned back and landed their troops at Moss and Son to march up to Oslo through the snow, so that their arrival, timed to correspond with the delivery of the ultimatum, would be delayed by several hours.

Von Falkenhorst was waiting for a visit from Major Quisling. He had sent for him several times, only to be told he was too busy. He heard the guard challenging someone at the door—he hoped it wasn't a messenger with further bad news. However it was not a German this time but a Norwegian who was escorted into his office. The general saw an unimpressive, untidily dressed man in a mackintosh, with thin sandy hair and pale-blue watery eyes, standing a couple of feet inside the doorway, nervously running a hand through his hair. He eyed the intruder sourly.

"Do you speak German?" he snapped.

"I do."

"Well, go and tell Major Quisling that I insist on seeing him at once. I have been waiting for over an hour."

"I am Major Quisling."

"You?" Von Falkenhorst could not hide his astonishment, and did not trouble to hide his disgust. Someone had made a bad mistake here, he thought. Unless this man had concealed qualities, which on closer inspection seemed unlikely. In his view, it was better to have an impressive-looking idiot as a leader than an insignificant genius. But the man Quisling appeared to be neither.

"Kindly explain why the Norwegians are fighting," he demanded, coldly.

Quisling strongly resented the General's discourtesy, and also his obvious contempt. He put a question of his own. "The Führer promised me the Germans would occupy the ports only," he said. "The administration of the rest of the country was to be left to me. But the *Blücher* carried hundreds of German civilians, sent to take over key posts practically everywhere in Norway. I heard this from survivors when she was sunk. What is your explanation?"

"You'd better take that up with the German Government," von Falkenhorst replied. "I'm only a soldier! But I suppose it was when you got this news that you instructed your fellow-countrymen to fight back? I will hold you personally responsible for the mass murder of hundreds of German soldiers and sailors. The Führer will hear of your disloyalty, you can be sure of that!"

This put Quisling in a quandary; he had no desire to admit to this contemptuous general that he had no influence whatever in Norway, so he searched his mind quickly for a scapegoat. "I am not responsible for the fighting," he said. "For this you must blame the King. His anti-German attitude is well known. And the people worship him; they would give their lives for him. I suggest that he should be found and killed, and then I shall be able to bring the Norwegians to their senses. If you are quick about it, the country should be under control before British troops are able to land. I took over the broadcasting station with some of my own men soon after your arrival, although the Defence Minister did unfortunately get a few minutes to put out an order for general mobilization. Since then, this order has been contradicted at regular intervals by my people. I have also just got control of the Oslo telephone exchange, so that Norway is now under a complete news blackout. This, of course, is in itself suspicious, so you should act as quickly as possible."

Was Quisling right about the King? Von Falkenhorst wondered. Possibly. He was certainly known to have great influence, and the fact that the Norwegians were resisting the Germans instead of welcoming them could well be his fault. Whether they would turn to this colourless man and accept his leadership instead was extremely doubtful, but with German backing he could probably be maintained as a figurehead in the eyes of the world. Indeed he would have to be since Hitler, inexplicably, had chosen him. The murder of the 67-year-old King Haakon would probably be a simple matter; nearly 6 feet

7 inches in height, the slim, soldierly figure with the huge black moustache was so well known that it would be extremely difficult to hide him for long. But the international implications of such an act would have to be considered; it might be wiser to take him prisoner. Another thought struck him: Quisling could well be covering up for his own mistakes. Why, for instance, were Norwegian volunteers getting to the front armed with rifles? The arrangement had been that Quisling should have all the recruiting depots destroyed as soon as the Germans landed; was he playing a double game? It was more than likely.

"Why didn't you destroy the mobilization centres as arranged?" he asked, suddenly.

"I did!"

"Then explain why the volunteers are armed."

"They have their own rifles. There was no way of getting those away from them—they all have them. Rifle-shooting is the favourite national sport in Norway, next to skiing. The rifle-clubs took over recruitment after I'd had the mobilization centres destroyed, but I've given orders for them to be blown up as well."

It was now clear to von Falkenhorst that the Germans had run into a hornets' nest. In the present weather conditions, a few hundred marksmen on skis who were familiar with the terrain could probably do more damage than a conventional army—in the short run. Yes, it was clearly the propaganda that was at fault.

"I will accept your explanation that the Norwegian King is to blame for the present state of affairs," he said, curtly. "He must be destroyed or captured as quickly as possible." And we should also try to capture the Prime Minister, he thought, so that he can be forced to broadcast to the people and tell them to lay down their arms; that will leave the country without official leaders, and the elevation of this little dimwit will be that much easier. He wrote for a time, and then looked up at Quisling, who was still standing, inwardly fuming. No one had offered him a chair.

"Go to the office of the newspaper with the largest circulation," he said, "and instruct the editor to print this memorandum from the German Government, explaining our actions, and telling the people what will happen to them if they don't cease resistance immediately. It was handed to the Norwegian Government some time ago by our Minister, Doctor Bräuer, but they threw it out—influenced probably, as you suggest, by King Haakon. However, if the whole nation should be allowed to read it, ordinary Norwegians might have the sense to stop fighting. You will have this printed, too." And he handed him the note that he had just finished writing. It stated that His Majesty King Haakon had criminally misled his people into believing that the Germans were their enemies, whereas their real enemies were the British; he was therefore a traitor to his country, and must be captured or killed. Anyone knowing anything of his whereabouts should contact the Oslo telephone exchange, when action would be taken immediately.

The editor of the *Oslo Dagblad* was slowly surfacing after the crowd in his office had thinned to one or two whispering groups. Ever since midnight he had been besieged by distraught people, either giving news or seeking it; the office telephones had never ceased ringing, and a gradual picture of what was actually happening in Norway during this disastrous night had been completing itself in his mind during the small hours. With the exception of Oslo, all the major ports—Bergen, Stavanger, Horten, Egersund, Kristiansand, Trondheim, Narvik —had been occupied simultaneously by the Germans under cover of darkness, and, judging by the sound of bombing at Fornebu Airport, the fall of the capital itself could not be long delayed. The Minister of Defence had got to the broad-casting station to order a general call-up just before Oslo Radio had been taken over, and His Majesty and the Government were leaving for Hamar, 60 miles north of Oslo, to avoid being captured while discussing their next moves. Conditions for mobilization were chaotic: most of the recruiting depots had been blown up, and Oslo Radio was putting out announcements every ten minutes instructing everyone to stay at home and not panic. If it wasn't for the rifle-clubs lending a hand, very few men would have been able to join up at all. As far as the Oslo district was concerned, men were beginning to arrive in fairly large numbers in the forests north of the town, fighting in groups as they went.

The time had now come for the editor to get the paper ready for printing, and to see that as much news and as few rumours as possible appeared in the *Dagblad*; this could well be its last uncensored edition for some considerable time to come—unless he managed to go underground.

As he sat checking the piles of reports that had come in, his latest visitor walked straight into his private office, leaving the door wide open. He was irritated by this lack of courtesy, an irritation which flared into anger as he recognized Vidkun Quisling. Nevertheless he forced himself to control his expression, and the tone in which he greeted his unwelcome guest was restrained; Quisling would doubtless provide some late news. It was just as he'd hoped. A piece of paper was thrown roughly on to the desk in front of him.

"Print that," ordered Quisling, briefly. The editor glanced up for a moment into the pale-blue misty eyes and saw that they were filled with bitterness and frustration.

"What is it?" he asked in a casual voice.

"It's a memorandum. A warning from the German Government telling Norwegians what will happen to them if they don't cease fighting immediately. And an order to them to co-operate. How they are to co-operate is set out here."

The editor pulled the document towards him. His trained eye had taken in the salient facts of the lengthy memorandum in thirty seconds flat. Then he re-read some of the clauses with a feeling of distinct satisfaction. Although the telephone exchange and broadcasting station had been taken over, the enemy clearly did not yet know that they had been just a little bit too slow over it. Both the British and French envoys, taking it for granted that their own telephone lines would be tapped, had been to see him some time ago to ask for help in contacting their governments with urgent messages; the replies were even at this moment in a locked drawer in his desk, decoded, waiting to be collected. The allies had offered to land troops at Molde and Andalsnes as quickly as possible; these two small ports were not among those taken by the enemy, and Andalsnes had the supreme advantage of being connected by road and rail to the capital, through the Roms Valley, the Gudbrands Valley and on south through Lillehammer to Oslo. Norway would not be fighting alone for long. It was also too late to forbid merchant ships to leave for foreign ports; nearly every ship in the merchant fleet, the fourth largest in the world, was already on her way to the nearest allied port. Military establishments and fortifications were to be handed over to the Germans intact. And pilots and lighthouse-keepers would place themselves at the disposal of the Germans. Like hell!

The rest of the document had a sickeningly familiar ring. Yes, he decided, he would certainly print this. If, owing to the confusing German broadcasts, there was the slightest doubt in any man's mind as to what he should do, the publication of these outrageous orders to a neutral country would dispel it.

"Very well," he said, in a deceptively mild tone, "I'll print it. Now leave me to get on with my work, and I'm sure your new masters are anxiously awaiting your return. Good night."

But Quisling hadn't finished. "You will also print this," he said savagely, slamming another document on to the table, "and you'd better remember to address me politely, or it'll be the worse for you. Tomorrow, I shall be Prime Minister of Norway."

The second document announced that King Haakon and his entire family were to be killed or taken prisoner. In the best interests of peace. Anyone who knew of their whereabouts should report at once. . . . The editor was appalled. The King would now be on his way to Hamar. Did Quisling know? The Government had included in their mobilization broadcast the fact that they intended to retire to Hamar for consultation, so anyone who could put two and two together. . . . When he had overcome his dismay, he realized that the sooner the whole nation was told of this threat to the King the better, firstly so that Norwegians everywhere could protect him if they saw him, and secondly because of the tremendous bitterness it would arouse against the Germans. Norwegians were slow to anger; nothing would stir them up faster than the deliberate, cold-blooded hounding to death of King Haakon, the symbol of their national liberty for the past thirty-five years, ever since they had finally thrown off the last remnants of Swedish domination and emerged a free nation. But he could not possibly, he decided, allow such an announcement to appear in the pages of the *Dagblad*—the paper would lose all credibility, and whatever he wrote during the inevitable occupation would be suspect.

Quisling noticed his hesitation and began to bluster. "You'll print that as well, whether you like it or not!" he shouted.

"No."

"Then I'll have you shot!"

"How would that help you? My staff wouldn't print it either."

"Then they'll be shot, too!" screamed Quisling.

"As you wish. But I doubt if German soldiers know how to print newspapers!" Quisling's behaviour suddenly put an idea into his head; it was worth trying. "Major Quisling," he said, quietly, using the old military title that everyone knew pleased Quisling, "in my opinion this announcement would come much better from you personally. It would—er—carry more authority, wouldn't it? Why don't you go down now to the broadcasting station and speak to the people yourself? After all, as you have just reminded me, you will be the Prime Minister tomorrow. And it's already well past midnight. You *are* the Prime Minister! So go and address your people."

As Quisling strutted from the office, the editor turned on his radio with a malicious grin. "Sing, little canary," he murmured, "sing your best. Tonight for the first time Norwegians will listen to you. And then you can just wait for one of them to come and wring your bloody neck!"

At half past six, von Falkenhorst and Lindauer listened to Quisling's speech on their radio. His voice was more impressive than his appearance, they decided; it would obviously pay to use him for official announcements, while keeping him in the background as much as possible otherwise. When he returned and asked what they had thought of his speech, the Germans were able to praise it quite sincerely.

"If the King were to decide to leave Oslo tonight," von Falkenhorst asked him, "where would he be most likely to go?"

"He'd probably go with the Government to Hamar; they're

on their way there already. If he manages to get to Hamar, he can go from there into Sweden, or across to the west coast, whichever he prefers."

Von Falkenhorst called an orderly. "Go and find Wing-Commander Goetz," he said. "Tell him to send a plane up to disrupt the traffic on the main road north from Oslo to Hamar. And then send me a report."

When the man had gone, he turned to Quisling.

"I'd like you to drive back to Oslo and put a heavy armed guard round the Bank of Norway," he said. "The merchant ships which were sent to take the gold bullion to Germany are still waiting to get past Dröbak. I can't think why the bloody garrison hasn't surrendered—we've been bombing them for hours. A few hours lost in our time-schedule in taking the capital didn't seem a very serious matter at first, but the side-effects are beginning to build up. In the first place, it was planned that our troops should already have been in Oslo when that Memorandum was delivered to the Norwegian Government, in which case they would have been obliged to accept it. But we weren't, and they've side-stepped. And now this idea of yours of capturing the King may not prove so easy; he'll get away if he's got any sense. . . . But don't put guards in the street round the Bank, or someone in authority may notice and begin to get ideas. You'll have to conceal your men in buildings adjoining the Bank—they must report at once if they see lorries being brought up to it, and if there's any activity of this kind we'll just have to send a few hundred troops straight up there in armoured cars to capture the building. And make a few discreet inquiries about the King while you're in Oslo."

When Quisling eventually returned, von Falkenhorst suffered a severe shock; the bullion had already gone. "How can you be sure?" he shouted. "You can't have got into the Bank."

"It wasn't necessary to get into the Bank; they've taken it all right. There were tracks of heavy lorries in the snow outside, and I followed them on foot to the junction with the main road north, but the tracks disappeared there. That road is completely choked with refugee traffic——"

"Have the chief constable of every town within a hundred

miles of Oslo arrested!" roared von Falkenhorst. "Bullion can only be hidden in a bank. Once the chief constables are here, we can begin to question them. . . . And the King?"

"I'm afraid he's left too."

NORTH FROM OSLO

TWO

THE GOLD OF A NATION VANISHES

WITH ITS POLICE ESCORT, the lorries, vans and trucks containing the eighty tons or so of Norwegian gold had set off in convoy on its way to Lillehammer, on the instructions of the Finance Minister, just as soon as the last van had been loaded and locked.

Olaf Larsen, who had been picked up by the police as an extra driver while running home to fetch his rifle, was sitting beside an elderly policeman in a milk-van, with a ton of gold on board the fragile vehicle. Like everyone else, he was in a state of nervous shock due to the suddenness of the invasion, and he was having a hard time trying to get hold of himself among complete strangers.

The convoy reached the junction with the main road; on it was an endless stream of private cars, all leaving the city for the mountains before it was too late. Without their police escort, it would have been impossible to break their way through the solid block of vehicles, but at the sight of the blinking blue lights the drivers swerved automatically to the side of the road; the policeman in the front escort car got out and held up the traffic to allow the whole convoy to get on to the main road, and they drove on past all the private cars until the road was clear before them. Then they gathered speed in an urgent attempt to reach Lillehammer before dawn. The snow did not greatly inconvenience the heavy lorries if driven carefully, but when the speed increased some of the overloaded little trucks skidded off the road. Each time this happened, the whole convoy had to stop.

Suddenly the lorry in front of Olaf's milk-van stopped again without warning. "Out, boy!" yelled the policeman. "Get under the van. Quick!"

Now what was the matter? He soon knew. An enemy plane was flying low along the road from the direction of

Oslo, machine-gunning the cars indiscriminately as it went.
Olaf had done blindly as he was told, and only just in time.
The hideous roaring of the plane as it flew overhead, leaving a trail of death and destruction behind it, had caused
panic.

Olaf was shaking like a leaf. He heard the plane returning.
With a roar and a hail of bullets it had gone again, and he
could hear screams and shouting from the civilian cars behind
them. They waited a little longer, and then the police escort
started to move up and down the line, checking for casualties
and damaged vehicles. One post office van was a complete
wreck—it had skidded into the ten-ton lorry in front of it,
and both its drivers were dead. By the time the convoy had
got under way again, some of the vehicles were dangerously
overloaded. They tried to increase speed, but this only resulted
in another truck skidding off the road, and further delay while
it was put back, and then, more slowly, they crept, freezing
and dead-tired, into Lillehammer.

The convoy was met by the chief constable and the local
bank manager; there was no chance for anyone to have a
rest yet. They were faced with the back-breaking task of
transferring the bullion from the vehicles to the bank vault.
Olaf worked on, hardly aware any more of what he was
doing, until at last someone came and told him to take a
break. He went inside the bank building and was given a
cup of coffee. But he put the cup down again immediately; he
found he was physically unable to drink. His throat muscles
were paralysed, and he could hardly breathe. The old men
watched him sympathetically.

"Cheer up, lad," ventured one. "We won't be occupied for
long, Hitler's bitten off more than he can chew this time."

"But we're unarmed!" wailed Olaf. "No planes, no guns—
nothing! We can't fight back!"

"Just as well," put in a grizzled veteran, briefly. "No sense
in getting every man killed, only to have to give in in the
end. Survival's the thing. As soon as the country's been taken,
we'll turn on the heat—like the people in all the other
countries the Germans have occupied. . . . Make every German
within two miles of you wish he'd never been born—that is,
the ones you don't manage to kill. They'll have to leave some

time—they can't occupy the world. Keep that in your head, boy, and tell your friends. What's your profession?"

"I'm an engineer," Olaf told him, in a more relaxed tone.

"An engineer, eh? Well, then, you'll be able to knock hell out of them, won't you?"

Much cheered by the opportunities for revenge that this speech conjured up, Olaf drank his coffee and returned to work. At last the unloading was finished, and the bank locked up. The police were to drive back to the capital to report the safe arrival of the gold to the Finance Minister, and they must be there before the Germans could get properly organized and notice their absence.

The chief constable noticed Olaf standing in the snow watching their departure, and took him into the manager's office for a drink. Both he and the bank manager offered to put him up, so that he could get a little sleep, but Olaf had been making his own plans while he was working, and told them that he had friends in Lillehammer called Bergstrom. If one of them would kindly drive him over, he and the Bergstrom boys could join up together.

"Kaare Bergstrom's boys?"

"That's right."

"I know them," said the chief constable. "I'll take you. There's just one thing, though, and that is that Oslo Radio doesn't normally start broadcasting till eight o'clock, and it's only just after seven, so it's quite likely that no one in Lillehammer knows there's a war on. People in the country go to bed early, so they won't have heard the special broadcasts; I knew nothing myself till the Finance Minister telephoned me. So I'll come in and tell them myself—it's going to be a great shock to them. . . . And not a word to them about the gold, mind; we'll probably get instructions to move it on again at dusk."

They rang the Bergstroms' bell, and after a fairly long wait Mrs Bergstrom appeared at the door in her dressing-gown.

"Why, Olaf Larsen!" she exclaimed, taking in the fact that he was in a filthy state and had arrived under police escort. "What can you have been up to?"

The chief constable answered her before Olaf got a chance. "He isn't in trouble, Mrs Bergstrom," he assured her, "but he's very tired. Have you got a spare bed for him? Once he's settled, I must have a talk with you and your husband."

"Very well," she said. "I'll call him down. All my boys are on holiday skiing in the mountains, so there's plenty of room. Olaf, go up to Peter and Rolf's room—you know where it is."

At nine o'clock, after only two hours' sleep in his office, the bank manager was awakened by loud shouting and the sound of angry protests in the street outside. He peered anxiously out of the window, and saw the chief constable being hustled into a car by several men and driven away. The mayor, who had apparently been summoned to his aid, was left sprawling in the road—one of the thugs had given him a sharp push as they drove off. The streets were full of people; news of the invasion had reached Lillehammer. He ran out into the snow and helped the mayor to his feet.

"What's going on?" he asked.

"Some of Quisling's men have got hold of the chief constable," the mayor told him. "They said he was 'wanted for questioning'. They wouldn't give me a reason, and as they were all armed there wasn't much I could do about it."

The bank manager could think of a good reason, but he kept it to himself. If the Germans were already looking for the gold reserves, and failed to get the information they wanted from chief constables, mayors would be their next target. However, with the chief constable gone, he realized that he was now the only person in Lillehammer who knew the gold was there, and he didn't see how he could maintain a continuous watch all alone. With the Government in hiding, it might be some days before they got around to sending further instructions.

And then he remembered the boy, Larsen. He wouldn't have been able to join up yet; although there were plenty of young men waiting, no recruiting officer had so far appeared in Lillehammer. Together the two of them would be able to guard the bank, watching and resting in turns. But an officer might arrive at any moment. . . . He got rid of the mayor as quickly as he decently could, and then snatched up the telephone book and looked up Kaare Bergstrom.

Mrs Bergstrom answered his call, and said quite firmly that

she would not dream of waking Olaf—he was quite exhausted. But something in the manager's tone made her change her mind, and she very reluctantly woke her guest.

"Come to the bank at once?" she heard Olaf say, sleepily. "What's the matter? Oh, I see. . . . Shall I bring my rifle?" He rang off, and asked Mrs Bergstrom if he could please have a cup of coffee; he was wanted at the bank.

"What for?" she demanded. "You've had practically no sleep."

Olaf, mindful of the chief constable's warning, murmured rather vaguely, "Government business of some kind. I'll be back."

"Not till you've had a good breakfast," she said.

It was nearly an hour before he reached the bank. There he listened to the manager's tale of woe with growing dismay. "But I was going to join up," he protested. "I want to go and fight."

"Thousands of men are going to fight. But you alone, besides myself, know that the gold reserves are here. Can't you see that your duty is to go on guarding the bank until it's taken off our hands?"

In spite of his frustration, Olaf saw that he was right. And then he remembered that Harald, Peter and Rolf Bergstrom were still skiing in the mountains. By the time they got news of the invasion and came back to volunteer, the gold would probably be on its way, and then they could all join up together as he had hoped. The bank manager was pleased when he heard this; now he could rely on the boy's co-operation for at least a couple of days.

"I'm going to lock the bank, and we'll guard it in turns," he said. "We'll put a couple of armchairs together and make a bed, and then one can sleep while the other keeps watch."

"We'll need some food and cigarettes," remarked Olaf. "And I'll have to tell Mrs Bergstrom. Shall I buy something?"

"Yes, do. If there's one thing I've got plenty of," said the manager with a grin, "it's money."

THREE

FOUR DAYS IN A COUNTRY BANK

WHILE THE KING, the Government and the gold reserves were in hiding somewhere in central Norway, the enemy were advancing relentlessly up the Gudbrands Valley from Oslo towards them, challenged only by the Second Division, whose ranks consisted chiefly of young men who had managed to get out of Oslo before the capital fell, and officers from all over the country who had been on leave in Oslo when the Germans landed. For the first few hours of fighting, they had been able to share the burden with the First Division, a regular peace-keeping force which had been stationed in the south-eastern tip of Norway, but they heard at dawn that the remains of that division, badly mauled, had gone over the border into Sweden and had been interned. The Second Division was now bearing the full brunt of the attack alone. The only other mobilized division in the country was the Sixth, a peace-keeping force in north Norway, but as there was no road of any kind between north and south Norway, it might as well have been on the moon. There was no news of the Third, Fourth or Fifth Divisions; in the present weather conditions, unusually harsh for the time of year, it was possible that they had been unable to mobilize at all.

General Headquarters had transferred themselves temporarily to Eidsvold, not very far north of Oslo; if they did not move again soon, they were likely to be overrun. Despatch riders arrived from them from time to time, but they did not give much information. The Germans, General Hvinden Haug was told again and again, were to be held at all costs to allow the King and Government to reach the west coast to be taken to safety by the allies, and so far the cost had been heavy. The front-line troops were mostly volunteers, some without military training, and they were tired out after twenty-four hours of continuous fighting; unless reinforcements arrived

in a very short time, those that remained of them were likely
to collapse from sheer exhaustion. If this happened, the Germans would pour over them, and there would be nothing to
prevent them from swarming across the country and seizing
the ports of Molde and Andalsnes from the rear before the
allies had had time to reach Norway at all.

The General knew that the recruiting depots were being
blown up all over the country. Nevertheless he considered that
by now something should have been arranged to get volunteers down to him from the Gudbrands Valley, stretching out
behind him nearly all the way across Norway; he bitterly
resented the lack of organization at headquarters.

Meanwhile he could take comfort from the fact that the
geographical and weather conditions had gone a long way
towards equalizing the struggle. Although the German field-
guns kept up an uninterrupted barrage, the actual shells were
doing little damage, since they were scarcely able to explode
at all in the thick snow. Low-level machine-gunning had been
abandoned; the pilots dared not fly too low over the never-
ending fir forests, and from higher up they could not see the
Norwegians, who were dressed in white coats and hoods. They
tried dropping incendiary bombs, but these simply fizzled out.
On the other hand the Germans, in their field-grey uniforms,
made splendid targets, and the front line had become a snipers'
paradise. If only, thought the General, I could get some fresh
troops, any fresh troops . . .

When darkness fell, the bombardment ceased abruptly. The
General assumed that the enemy had decided to take cover
from the cold, and he gave orders that men were to be
sheltered during the hours of darkness wherever possible, in
farms, outhouses, lumber-camps—anywhere, rather than let
them freeze to death.

When he returned to his makeshift tent, he found two
more despatches waiting for him; help was at last at hand.
The first was from the Minister of Defence, announcing the
appointment of a new Commander-in-Chief, Colonel Otto
Ruge, and the second was from Ruge himself, containing a
list of officers to be sent to him immediately to form his new
staff, and informing the Second Division that he had turned
Lillehammer into a mobilization centre. All men, supplies

and equipment were massing there, and Major Ording was to be sent up at once to take charge. It was signed "Otto Ruge, G.O.C.-in-C.". The General suddenly felt cheerful. Although in his seventies, Ruge was not a man to let the grass grow under his feet; improvements could be expected from now on. He had already been Commander-in-Chief of the Army, and was still Inspector-General of the Infantry, and had the reputation of being a master-strategist. His despatch had come from Minnesund, where he was at present busy training recruits for the Royal Guard; it appeared that he intended to stay there for the time being—Minnesund was a long way behind the lines, nearly as far north as Hamar.

Of the officers requested by Otto Ruge, Major Arne Ording was the first to arrive. He was a man who had spent the better part of his life campaigning with foreign armies all over the world. His cynical smile gave the impression of a man who, at forty-five, had precious little faith left in anything. Today, however, he was not smiling; he was filled with anger and an intense bitterness at this sudden unprovoked attack upon his homeland to which he had only recently returned.

"Well?" he asked sharply.

"Ording," said the General, "we have a new Commander-in-Chief, Otto Ruge; his first despatch has just arrived. He's making arrangements to have reinforcements sent to the front at once. And he's given orders for everyone within range to be sent to Lillehammer. You are to be sent to take charge. Volunteers and the contents of other armouries are all to be sent there, and they are to be sorted out and sent down to this front on the double."

At that moment, Captain Johan Olsen entered the tent. He had to stoop to get in, and once inside his huge presence practically filled it.

"Council of war?" he asked briefly.

"Orders from the new Commander-in-Chief, General Ruge," the General told him.

"Ruge? Magnificent! Now things ought to get moving. When's he sending reinforcements, sir?"

"Immediately. They're all to come from Lillehammer, and Ording's going up to take charge. You, Olsen, have been chosen for his own staff at Minnesund. You're to take three lieutenants with you—the despatch says you can pick your own men. You'd better get off at once. The senior officers he's asked for will follow as soon as possible—you can't pull three colonels out of the front line without making adjustments."

"Right, sir, I'm off," said Olsen, almost before the General had finished speaking. "Arne, if you're taking over at Lillehammer, you'd better send any untrained men to us at Minnesund, and we'll give them a lick and a promise."

Arne Ording reached Lillehammer shortly after daybreak. A professional soldier, he was used to going without sleep, but even he was beginning to feel the effects of the insidious cold. He was considerably heartened by the sight of hundreds of young men walking about the town. Arrived at the recruiting office, he strode straight in, and was surprised to find old Colonel Ole-Jacob Broch sitting at a desk, poring over a pile of papers.

"Hallo, there," he greeted him. "I thought you'd retired."

"I had," replied the tubby little Colonel, equably, "but I put on my uniform and drove across to see what was going on. I found nobody here, so I took over myself."

Ording put his cap on the table and sat down. "Good for you!" he said, grinning.

The Colonel looked nettled. "I may be old, Major," he said sharply, "but at least I know how to recruit men. I've recruited 600 already—in fact, it was lucky I came when I did, because some of them had been hanging about for some time and were beginning to go off again. I was going to send them down to the front—I've collected enough buses for them, and they've all got their own rifles—but there's only one thing that's holding me up, and that is that there's no key to the armoury, so I can't give them any spare ammunition. The chief constable had the key, but he was kidnapped by Quisling's thugs early yesterday morning——"

"Well, go and shoot the lock off at once, for Christ's sake!" exclaimed Ording. "This is *war*, man—not a military exercise!"

Arne sat down, and someone brought him a cup of coffee. "Just up from the front, sir?" asked the man, respectfully.

c

"That's right."

"What's it like down there?"

Arne glanced round, and saw that some twenty or thirty men had crowded into the office and were listening; it wouldn't do to discourage them. "Cold," he said, "but there's plenty of game if you're a good shot!"

He had the satisfaction of hearing bus after bus starting up and driving off, and by the time Colonel Broch returned triumphant he was sound asleep.

For three whole days Olaf Larsen remained in Lillehammer, taking turns with the bank manager to guard the gold reserves and fretting at the delay. At first they had expected the Government to send instructions about the bullion at any moment, but as time passed they had gradually begun to wonder whether a message would come at all.

On the first day, Olaf had gone back to the Bergstroms' when it was his turn to rest, but when he came back again on the second day, he noticed a change in Mr Bergstrom's attitude. Although Mrs Bergstrom believed him when he said he was on government business, he soon realized that Mr Bergstrom most emphatically did not. He mentioned once or twice that there was no point in Olaf waiting for his sons, as they might have joined up somewhere else, and thereafter refused to speak to his guest at all. His attitude hurt Olaf acutely—if only he had managed to join up in Oslo, he thought, he would never have landed himself in this mess. The bank manager was becoming more and more irritable; he was obsessed with his responsibility, and even when Olaf was on watch he could get no rest. He just sat by the telephone all day and most of the night, waiting for the call that never came.

Olaf had soon discovered that Lillehammer had become a mobilization centre, and he felt uncomfortably conspicuous in his civilian clothes. The curious looks that followed him as he wandered about the town embarrassed him, but he had nowhere to hide except at the bank or at the Bergstroms', where he was ignored.

On the afternoon of the 12th, he was staring into shop windows, miserably depressed, when suddenly he felt strong arms round his waist, and a deep voice called, "Got you!" He was thrown into the air, turned round and set down on his feet facing his captor.

"Oh, Harald!" he cried, angrily. "How *could* you give me such a fright?"

"Sorry to scare you," said Harald Bergstrom, grinning down at him. "I thought you'd be glad to see me."

"Of course I am! I was beginning to think you were never coming. Are you all back?"

"Yes, all of us. And I've been looking for you for about two hours. Father told us you were in Lillehammer; he thinks you've gone batty!"

"I know," said Olaf, ruefully, "or worse. Oh, Harald, it's good to see you! I thought you must have all joined up somewhere else. When did you arrive?"

"Just after lunch. We didn't hear about the war till yesterday evening—the twins went down the mountain to buy some stores, and they came back with the news. Luckily the buses are still running; we skied down to the main road early this morning and caught one. . . . But you must tell me what all this secrecy is about."

Olaf was hustled into a cafe, one huge hand propelling him through the doorway, and Harald ordered coffee. "Now then," he said.

"Harald," said Olaf, desperately, "I can't tell you any more than I've told your father, which is that I'm waiting for instructions."

"What about?" he asked.

"I'm not allowed to say." Olaf's mouth was set in an obstinate line; Harald was puzzled. He contemplated the boy for a few moments—he certainly appeared to be under strain.

"Just who are you expecting instructions from?"

"The Government," replied Olaf, unwillingly.

"But, you silly little sod, the Government are in hiding! Don't you know that the Germans are looking for them and the King in order to murder them? It was announced on the radio—Dad's given us all the news. Hamar, Elverum and Nybergsund have already been bombed because they were seen there, although each time they managed to get away. They haven't been heard of for two days; you don't think they're going to risk being caught just to communicate with you, do you? What's it all about, anyway? If the Government can trust you with a secret, they can trust me. So out with it!"

Olaf looked up into the stern face of the elder brother of his friends, hesitated for a moment, and then took a deep breath; Harald leaned forward expectantly. But then the light of conspiracy died in Olaf's eyes. "It's not my secret," he muttered.

"I just don't know what to make of you," Harald said, grimly. "Finish your coffee, and come home and see the others."

Peter and Rolf were delighted to see Olaf; they were both full of talk about joining the army and having a bash at the Germans, and could hardly wait to present themselves at the recruiting office. The only disgruntled member of the family was Björn, who, at sixteen, would have to be left behind.

"Well, Björn," said his father, rather caustically, "at least you'll have someone to keep you company—Olaf Larsen's not joining up either."

They all turned to stare incredulously at Olaf. "I'll just go out again and see if any instructions have come for me yet," he managed to say, making hurriedly for the door.

"Björn," whispered Rolf, "Olaf's got something going—I'm sure of it. Get after him, and let us know what he's up to."

Björn, a gawky, six-foot teenager, was hardly the ideal spy, but Olaf was too preoccupied to notice that he was being followed. Just as he was about to cross the road to the bank, a crowd of strangers walked out of it. He froze in horror—the only thought in his mind was that the bank manager was being kidnapped, and he was alone and could do nothing to help. To his tremendous relief and satisfaction, he recognized the Prime Minister. Without pausing to think, he ran straight across the road to him. "Sir," he panted, "have you come about the gold?"

The group of men stopped, and they all glared at Olaf. "Who the devil are you?" demanded the Prime Minister, sharply, unexpectedly producing a pistol from his pocket. The other men closed in round Olaf; he was trapped. He realized too late that he should never have approached these men; from the look of them, he guessed they were all cabinet ministers, and after several days on the run they would be liable to shoot a suspicious stranger on sight. He gulped. "My—my name's Olaf Larsen," he began. "I——"

But it wasn't necessary to say any more. The Prime Minister had put his gun back into his pocket and was smiling and holding out his hand to him. "How do you do, young man?" he said, kindly. "The bank manager has told me about you. I'm very glad to have this opportunity of thanking you for all you've done so far. If you want to help to get the country's gold to the coast, go in and see him now; he's just been told what's been planned."

Björn Bergstrom watched with tremendous interest. As soon as Olaf had entered the bank he made for home, and reported to Rolf everything he had seen.

FOUR

THE ARMY STEPS IN

GENERAL RUGE, still training troops at Minnesund, was handed a telephone message when he walked into his office at about four o'clock that afternoon. The call, recorded at three o'clock, was from the Minister of Finance, and he had been speaking from Lillehammer. Ruge was asked to send up immediately a responsible officer to organize and supervise an undertaking of great national importance. All details would be given to the officer personally at Lillehammer. He would send his best officer, Johan Olsen, he decided, and if it was a false alarm, he could always come back. He had proved tremendously useful during the past three days, making soldiers of some kind out of the endless stream of young men that Arne Ording was sending across from Lillehammer, and, apart from that, he enjoyed his company. He sent an orderly to fetch him.

When Johan entered the office, he showed him the message. "What d'you make of that?" he asked.

"He's probably lost his briefcase," replied Johan, flippantly.

Ruge grinned. "Well, whatever's the matter, I want you to go and sort it out," he said. "If it's a false alarm, you can just come back. And if it's important, let me know immediately. Either way, the sooner you get going, the better. And good luck to you."

An hour later, Johan reached Lillehammer. He drove straight to the recruiting office, sought out Arne Ording, and showed him the message.

"Ruge wants this looked into on the double," he said. "D'you know anything about it?"

"I'm afraid I don't," said Arne, "but I expect Colonel Broch does, he's been at the bank most of the day. Some of the cabinet ministers arrived here from Nybergsund, by what appears to have been a very circuitous route, and now Broch's

sent them over west—to Lesjaverk, actually. It's too dangerous to have them here; they could have been followed, and
we can't allow our only mobilization centre to be bombed—
not until the allies land, anyway."

"Was the King here?"

"No, he wasn't. Actually——"

"What on earth's Ole-Jacob Broch giving orders for?"
demanded Johan, interrupting him. "He must be nearly
eighty!"

"I'm sixty-five," came a somewhat acid voice from behind
him, and added, as Johan started to apologize, "No time for
the courtesies, Olsen. Ording and I are both extremely worried;
the Government's lost touch with the King and the Crown
Prince."

"What! Between here and Nybergsund?"

"Apparently. The cars were being driven very far apart, so
as not to be too noticeable from the air. The royal cars were
at the back. A few soldiers of the Royal Guard are with them,
and four or five of the ministers——"

"But why hasn't Ruge been told? This is extremely serious."

"You don't have to tell us that, Johan," said Arne, "but it's
only just happened. They sent a message two days ago to say
that they were all coming to Lillehammer, but only about
half of them actually turned up. The ones who came here
were in a terrible state—they'd been back along the road
looking for the King for more than twenty-four hours."

"D'you think the Germans have got him?" asked Johan,
anxiously.

"Not a chance. They'd be yelling themselves hoarse if they
had! But he must be extremely well hidden, if neither ourselves nor the enemy have managed to get a sniff of him in
forty-eight hours."

"I'm surprised no one's reported him to the Oslo exchange
yet."

Arne laughed. "That idea of Quisling's has backfired. It
worked on the first day, and they nearly caught the lot of
them, but since then the whole country's taken a hand, and
reports have been coming through from everywhere to say
the King's been seen. The exchanges were told to put all the
calls through, so the Oslo exchange has been swamped. Even

the Germans can see that he can't be in twenty places at once, so they'll just have to think up something else."

"They will! But in the meantime, the King must be found; if a ship comes in for him, he's got to be told at once, hasn't he?"

"We've been telephoning all over the place," Broch told him, "but no one seems to have seen him. All telephone exchanges have been alerted in the area, but no one's reported back yet."

"D'you mean you've been telephoning quite openly all round the district reporting that you've lost touch with the King?"

"Well, how else d'you suggest we find him?"

"But supposing one of those exchanges were to fall into enemy hands?"

"Suppose, suppose, suppose!" growled the colonel. "There's simply nothing else to be done. Is this a social visit, or did you have a special reason for calling?"

"I had, sir, yes. It's this." And he handed over the copy of the Finance Minister's telephone call. "Any idea what this is about?"

Colonel Broch took it and read it. His face changed, and he looked up sharply. "This message was sent to Ruge hours ago," he said. "Why didn't you come at once?"

"We're extremely busy at G.H.Q.," replied Johan, equally sharply. "Ruge's short-staffed. He told me to sort this out and get back to him as quickly as possible."

"But, my dear chap!" Broch stared at him. "Didn't either of you realize from the way it's worded, that this was a matter of the first importance?"

"No. We thought it would be just some government mix-up. After all, the Minister of Finance has nothing to do with the army. But if it's important, you'd better tell me at once what's the matter."

The colonel glared at him. " 'The matter', as you call it, Olsen," he stated, "is, quite bluntly, this: the entire assets of the Bank of Norway are at present in the local branch here at Lillehammer, and must somehow be got out of danger at once. The stuff was brought up here from Oslo by the police when the Germans landed; the Government asked the British envoy if he could have it shipped to England, but since then they've made no further arrangements. Today at last they have told us (or, rather, me), that it's here, and gone off leaving orders that it must somehow be got to the west coast. That, Olsen, is the 'undertaking of great national importance' referred to in this message, that you are requested to—and again I quote—'organize and supervise'."

Johan stared at him for a full half-minute. "As you say," he said, "they have certainly left it very late in the day; the Germans are only five miles south of Minnesund! But I would have thought it would have been better simply to burn it; then no unauthorized person could use it. The Government can easily print some more when they get to England. There's no point in taking it anywhere. After all, it's only paper."

"It's *not* paper! It's gold. Gold bullion. All the gold the country possesses." The colonel shrugged helplessly.

"Do you mean to say," exclaimed Arne, "that they've sent several tons of gold bullion to be looked after by a country bank manager, and then forgotten all about it?"

"Not exactly forgotten, Ording, but, shall we say, 'failed to make further contact'," said the colonel drily. "The Prime Minister's arrangements with the British envoy, as regards landing troops and sending in ships to take off the King, the Crown Prince, the Government and the gold, were all made at Hamar, but they've been closely pursued by the enemy ever since, and given no time to think, and the bullion is still lying here. That message of yours, Olsen, to General Ruge was sent on the Finance Minister's instructions, after they had all had a long talk with me and the bank manager; then, just as they were standing on the doorstep of a hotel, a reconnaissance plane flew over, and they all left immediately, without waiting for Ruge's answer."

"I should have thought that at this late stage," said Johan, "it would really be better to leave the stuff where it is, because the Germans would never guess that anyone in authority could be so daft. . . . Unless, of course," he added, suddenly alert, "there's any reason to suppose that they're on the track of it already?"

"That, Olsen," was the answer, "is unfortunately just the point. As you say, they would never guess, because they'd never dream of doing anything so offhand themselves, but it is known for certain that they are already looking for it. The Prime Minister told me he had got a message from the Oslo police while the Government were at Nybergsund saying that the enemy had been to the Bank of Norway in Oslo and found the vaults empty. Immediately this came to be known on the morning of the 9th, it appears that Quisling sent men from Oslo to as many towns as could be reached before the towns- people realized that the country was at war, and kidnapped their chief constables. They can question these men at their leisure, when they've occupied the country, and I'm sorry to say that Lillehammer's chief constable is on the list. So you see, the gold can't stay where it is, can it?"

As soon as Johan heard this, any hope that he had enter- tained that the Finance Minister had got into a panic over nothing evaporated. "Are you quite sure they haven't managed to get the information out of the chief constable of Oslo already?" he asked anxiously.

"I know they tried. But they didn't succeed. As the Oslo police were all back in the capital before the Germans noticed their absence, they accepted that they knew nothing about it, and are assuming that the army are responsible for having moved the bullion. But they also know that no allied ships have so far arrived to take it out of their reach, and they will easily have checked that the Swedes haven't got it."

"Well," said Johan determinedly, "there's absolutely no time to lose. Can you get hold of the bank manager?"

The bank manager got the Colonel's telephone message with great satisfaction—at last things were moving. Colonel Broch introduced him to Captain Olsen, and he looked at him hope- fully. "So you're going to take the gold to safety?" he said.

Put thus baldly, the gigantic difficulties that would beset such an undertaking suddenly appeared immeasurable; for a moment, Johan was daunted. Then he noticed that they were all looking at him anxiously.

"I can but try," he said, "although how on earth I am to get it to the west coast and on to a ship when I don't know which port the allies will land at or when is, you'll admit, something of a problem."

"The police used lorries," the bank manager told him.

"Once it's out of Lillehammer, you could hide somewhere until you get further instructions. The Germans could be here any time now."

"How many lorries were used to bring it up?"

"About thirty-five vehicles altogether, of all shapes and sizes. There's over 80 tons of bullion."

"As much as that! Well, I certainly can't use lorries," said Johan, decidedly. "A midnight dash is one thing, but I'll have to be waiting around for some days. I'd look like a travelling circus; every spotter plane in the country would be on my tail in five minutes. No, I think the only possible thing would be a train—a goods train, if one can be got, that can be hidden away in out-of-the-way sidings. But if this job is to be done at all, it must be done immediately. I'll get back down to Minnesund at once and discuss things with Ruge, and I'll tell him about the King while I'm about it. Expect me back in about two hours."

Ruge watched Johan Olsen as he strode purposefully towards him across the parade-ground.

He listened in silence while Johan made a full report; his first remark when he finally spoke was not about the gold but about the King. "As far as His Majesty is concerned," he said, "I can set your mind at rest. He's somewhere between Rendal and Alvdal—I know the exact farmhouse. He telephoned me just after you left this afternoon."

"He took that risk?"

"It wasn't a risk; one of the few things I managed to arrange during my brief interview at Elverum was a code-name for him—I felt this to be an absolute necessity, so that he could ask me for help at any time. His code-name is 'Magnus'."

"Well, that's certainly good news! How is he?"

"Very tired; he's resting. They lost touch with the others when one of the cars got a puncture, and decided to take a short cut to catch up. Fatal thing to do in this weather in the mountains. Also, they were seen, and parachute troops were landed in Rendal. The Germans were all mopped up by the local farmers, but I gather the royal party have had a pretty bad time."

"Why don't they just cross into Sweden?"

"They can't, Johan. They inquired, of course, but were told that if they did so they would be interned. We have to re-member that Sweden may be in the war too, at any moment, and there's absolutely no indication as to which side she would join. And if Sweden went in with the Germans, where would the King be then? No, the allies must take him to England as they promised. . . . But we'll get back to his problems in a moment. Our gold reserves, you say, have been dumped at Lillehammer! They never even mentioned that to me; there was so much to discuss when I took over——"

" 'Dumped' is the word sir! I've—er—been thinking how to rescue the stuff; there's so little time."

"Less than you know, actually! The Germans gained another mile or so this afternoon. They flew in reinforcements." He smiled. "Do I gather from your attitude that you're volunteer-ing to take charge of the gold yourself?"

"Well, yes, sir—I'd rather taken it for granted! But if——"

Ruge held up his hand. "No 'ifs'! You're the man I'd choose, and I'm glad you want to go. But you've been so busy on the training side that there hasn't been a chance to talk to you about overall strategy; I'll have to put you in the picture now, so that you'll be able to plan your route to the west coast, and take evasive action. But first of all, how do you propose to carry the bullion without attracting the attention of our friends in the sky? Their reconnaissance planes can go where they like; we've nothing to put up against them."

"I thought a train would be best, sir—a goods train. I could only use lorries if I could travel straight across the country without stopping and be sure of a ship when I reached the coast."

"I'm afraid there's absolutely no chance of your having it as easy as that—the allies haven't even landed yet, so you can't go and hang about at either Molde or Andalsnes. You'll have to circle round for a bit, probably for several days. I see your objection to lorries, but you'll have to be extremely cautious with a train, because they've been dropping parachute troops in a good many places. As far as the King is concerned, they can't catch him that way, as sharpshooters all over the country are protecting him as he moves from place to place, but if you ran into a group of them with a train it might be a different story. They could take over your train and drive it to Bergen or to Trondheim, or even back to Oslo."

"But would they take any interest in an ordinary goods train, if their orders were to capture the King?"

"That, of course," agreed Ruge, "is your strongest argument for taking a train; lorries could so easily be ambushed and searched. But I gathered from what you said that they were already looking for the gold."

"They've arrested a lot of chief constables, yes. But I've been thinking, and I was relying partly on the timing of my trip to get me by. After all, the Germans are very logical; I was hoping they would assume that the gold had been hidden somewhere already, in which case they could look for it at their leisure once Norway had been occupied, or else that it had already been taken to the west coast for shipment. They'd hardly expect us to bury it for four days and then suddenly dig it up again!"

Ruge stood up. "A train would appear, at any rate, to be making the best of a bad job," he said. "I can only wish you luck—you'll need it! If the gold is left in Lillehammer, they'll certainly find it, and if you move it at once you *might* just get it through. So naturally it's worth a try. Now come over here and take a look at this map."

Johan followed him across the room to where a large map hung on a wall, with a lot of flags pinned into it. "You already know the Germans are coming inland from Oslo," began Ruge. "They are also coming inland from Trondheim. At the moment, that front is threatening Stören. Here." And he pointed with his cane. "Fifth Division are slowly mobilizing north of Stören, and are offering what resistance they can. Fourth Division is over on the west. Here. Their orders are to keep the ports of Molde and Andalsnes clear for allied landings. Third Division is down near Stavanger. Here. I can't use them at the moment, because they're boxed in; neither can I use Sixth Division in north Norway.

"Now if these two invading forces continue inland from Oslo and Trondheim the way they are doing, they will eventually meet at Dombas. Here." And he pointed to a town about three-quarters of the way up the Gudbrands Valley.

"If the two German spearheads should succeed in joining forces at Dombas before the King and the Government—and now the gold—get through to the west, you'll all be caught in a trap. There is no passable road at this time of the year to Andalsnes and Molde except up the Gudbrands Valley and out to the coast through the Roms Valley; the King and his ministers can't be expected to ski across mountains, and you certainly can't take several tons of gold that way either. The Germans know all this, and they are keeping a very sharp lookout between Dombas and the west coast. So you'll have to hang about somewhere within reach, and get through to the coast at the last moment. In fact, it's a race between the allies and the Germans for Dombas. Are you with me?"

"I am, indeed! But I'll have to pick up information as I go, so as to know where and when to move; once I've left Lillehammer, I'll be entirely isolated."

"Yes, you will. But now that you know where our own troops are, you might be able to take cover with them for a bit if things get really hot. If you need help, don't hesitate to ask for it. No messing. Understood . . .? Now I'm going to give you a code-name as well. You can be 'Fridtjof'. I'll inform all divisional commanders, and also Colonel Hagen, in command of marines at Andalsnes; he'll know what arrangements the allies are making. If anyone can pull this off, Johan, you can. Arne Ording's still at Lillehammer, isn't he?"

"Yes, sir."

"Well, tell him he is to take some men and drive over at first light and join His Majesty and escort him to the west coast; he has too few soldiers with him. He refused to have more, as he said that every man was needed at the front, but I have persuaded him that it would have an appalling effect on morale if he were to be killed or captured, so he has agreed to accept more guards." He pointed to the map once more with his cane. "He is exactly here," he said, "at the moment; about five miles north of Rendal, as you see. He is at a farm owned by a man called Wolff. He has promised to wait for an escort."

"I'll tell Ording, sir."

"Right. And tell Colonel Broch that he's to carry on sending recruits to the Second Division until the enemy starts threatening Lillehammer itself, and then he's to take all the men and arms he has there and take up a new position at Dombas. . . . Well, goodbye, Johan, and good luck. This constant retreating is hard to bear, but it's all we can do till help comes."

Alone with his problem as he drove back to Lillehammer, Johan's mood varied from hopefulness to gloomy despair. He realized that if he didn't get going at once he had no hope of success whatsoever. He drove fast, and reached Lillehammer in a snowstorm. Broch and Ording were waiting for him in the recruiting office.

"Well?" asked Arne. "What was his reaction to a train?"

"Qualified," replied Johan. "But he couldn't think of anything better! And now, I've got some good news for you. Ruge knows exactly where His Majesty is, so you can stop worrying. And I've got special orders for both of you."

Arne's eyes sparkled when Johan gave him his orders from General Ruge. He had resigned himself to rejoining the Second Division when it reached Lillehammer, and then just carrying on with the disheartening retreat before the invading army through the snow. Broch was also pleased with the instructions as to his future activities; he was particularly glad that Ruge seemed just to have taken it for granted that he was back in the army, and with his old rank. Johan told them about the German spearhead coming inland from Trondheim, and that Colonel Hagen of the marines at Andalsnes was the man to contact for news of the allies. And he told them the two code-names.

"I'll carry on training as many men as possible when I get to Dombas," said Broch, happily. "I might even be able to form a strong-point there, as it's obviously a key position, and maybe even hold the town myself for a little while if necessary." Tired though he was, he was excited by the possibility of actually being able to lead troops into battle.

"I didn't know you could drive a train, Johan," remarked Arne.

"Drive it? Christ, I'll have to start thinking about details! This thing has got to be, as the message said, organized as well as supervised! I'll need an armed crew, and I shouldn't think rifles will be enough to defend ourselves and our cargo if the Germans get wind of us. Would you have a few machine-guns to spare for me, Colonel?"

"Of course, my boy, of course!" beamed Broch. "But the first and most important thing to do is to try and get you a train. I'll go straight over now and have a word with the station-master."

Arne and Johan then settled down to discuss practical details, and, as a definite plan began to emerge, Johan found his feeling of apprehension gradually being replaced by one of pleasurable anticipation. The bank manager dropped in to see how things were going, and to find out whether a decision had been come to as to how the gold was to be carried.

"Broch's gone off to see whether he can find a goods train," Johan told him. "It certainly seems the most suitable method of carrying such a cargo. Or," he amended, "the least unsuitable. The whole scheme still seems somewhat mad to me."

"An off-the-cuff plan like this probably has a better chance of success than any amount of careful preparation, I should think," said the bank manager, encouragingly. "The madder the better, to have any hope of getting away with something when the Germans are after you."

Johan suddenly grinned. The audacity of the thing appealed to him.

When the station-master was acquainted with the problem, his eyes widened. "I think I can get you a goods train," he said. "But who's going to do the loading? We've only got one porter left; the others have joined the army."

"The town's full of recruits."

"Well, that should take care of that one. But how much gold is there? I mean, how many trucks would you want?"

They all looked at the bank manager. "Even I can't say definitely," he said. "I should say there is between 80 and 85 tons of bullion."

The station-master was shocked at such vagueness, but said tactfully that this gave him a general idea.

"You must add an extra truck for me and my men to sleep in," Johan told him, "and I'll need a man to drive the thing."

"The train I have in mind already has a driver."

When the station-master had gone, the Colonel asked Johan what his plans were for tonight.

"I thought Hjerkinn would be best for the first night," he said. "I can drive through Dombas and go on up north from there into the mountains. Hjerkinn looks from the map to be the only place around there large enough to have a good choice of sidings, and the following day I'll have time to look for somewhere better if necessary. I don't want to move about too much. But I must get hidden before dawn, or I won't stand a chance."

"You're right. I gathered from the ministers who came here that the spotter planes were getting rather desperate," said Broch. "You'd better say at once what you think you'll need, and I can see that you get it."

Having discussed this with Arne already, Johan was able to answer this promptly, too. "I'll need a dozen men or so, besides myself and the driver," he said, "and food and cigarettes for us all for at least a week; I don't want to have to send men wandering off on forage hunts if I can help it. Also two machine-guns, one for each end of the train, with ammunition, and a couple of submachine-guns, and some hand-grenades, and plenty of rifle bullets and a few spare rifles. And bedding and medical kit—and make sure that includes brandy and schnapps! Also skis and snow-shoes. Oh, and we'll need a well-shaded hurricane lamp, and a supply of paraffin for it. And please don't be stingy with the food! We'll get water at the stations . . ." He stood up and stretched. "I think I'm going to enjoy this," he said with a sudden grin. "I'd like to choose my men now. Where's the best place to go for volunteers?"

"The theatre," Broch told him. "We've got about 800 men all kitted up waiting for their buses to take them straight down to the front, but there should still be about 200 left. Ording and I have been resting them on arrival, as some of them have skied in from quite long distances. You should find plenty to choose from in the theatre. And I agree with you, I'm sure you'll enjoy it—I only hope you succeed. At least it's something positive to do, rather than just trying to see how long one can hold out. By the way, there's a Sergeant with the men; I expect you'll find him a help."

"What's he like?"

"You'll see," said the old man, grinning rather maliciously.

D

As Johan turned to go, the station-master returned, breath-less. "I've got a goods train for you," he announced proudly, "but the engine's dead cold. The driver wants someone to help him stoke it."

Colonel Broch said he would send someone at once, and Captain Olsen told him to tell the driver to be prepared to leave in an hour.

"Good Lord!" exclaimed the station-master. "Have you no idea how a train works? You have to get up a tremendous head of steam to make it move. That takes time."

"How much time?"

"About two hours, usually. But with the weight this one will be carrying, probably more."

"I'll expect it to be ready in two hours."

"It'll take longer than that, I'm afraid. You've got to con-sider the time all that loading will take."

"We can load while the engine's being stoked."

"No, sir. I'm sorry, but you can't; the train's lying in a siding—it'll have to be moved to the goods-shed first, so that you can load from a platform. The bullion will be packed in boxes; it'll take two or three men to lift each box."

Johan began to see the hours stretching out before him, but, whatever the difficulties, it was absolutely essential to get to his destination while it was still dark.

"At least men can be bringing the gold from the bank to the goods-shed for loading while the driver's fiddling with his engine," he said. "That would save time."

"It would, indeed," agreed the station-master with relief. "You can borrow the goods trolleys; we've got three of them. They'll have to be wheeled all the way down the road and across the square to the bank. You'll need armed guards, I should think. How many men can be spared?"

"You can borrow as many recruits as you like, Olsen," said the Colonel. "I'll keep back a couple of bus-loads. They can go on down to the front when they've finished."

"In that case," said the station-master, "they should be ready to load by the time the train's got steam up. With un-limited manpower, you should only need another hour or so for loading up, and about ten minutes for putting the train on to the right line. Where are you going, by the way?"

"Hjerkinn. How long will it take me to get there?"

"You might do it in five hours nonstop, if you're lucky."

"Well, it's nine o'clock now," said Johan, "so that means we should get in at about—let's see—half past five in the morning. It's cutting it extremely fine. Everyone will just have to be as quick as they can, that's all. Does the driver need a permanent stoker?"

"Oh, yes, sir. Your driver's got one, actually, but he's just having a few hours off. He'll be back in good time before you leave."

"He'll have to be left behind; I can't have my train cluttered up with civilians. I can allocate stokers. Is it difficult to stoke?"

"Not really, as long as the men do what the driver tells them. They'll soon get the hang of it."

"I'll supervise the loading," said the Colonel. "You get off now and choose your team. The sooner you get out of here, the better. I have a feeling it won't be long before Lillehammer gets its first air raid. When you've picked your men, come back and see how we're getting on."

"Captain Olsen," said the bank manager, "there's a young man here who came up with the gold from Oslo. He's been waiting anxiously ever since the first night to hear what's to be done with it, and he's been a great help to me. I couldn't have guarded the bullion without him. So will you please say whether you want to take him with you, or else let him join the army."

"Tell me where he is; I'll see him at once."

FIVE

WESTWARD BOUND IN A GOODS TRAIN

OLAF'S SPIRITS had risen amazingly now that the problem of the gold was at last in hand, and the talk and laughter in the sitting-room of the Bergstroms' house was so loud that the bank manager had to knock on the door several times before being heard. When he asked for Olaf Larsen, and it was seen that he was accompanied by an army Captain, there was great excitement. As he went off with them, Björn followed as before, and then came running back to say that the Captain had taken Olaf with him to the theatre, where they knew that a lot of men would be waiting to be sent to the front.

"Well done, Björn!" cried Harald. "He'll have gone to ask for volunteers for whatever it is. So that's where *we're* going too! And you'd better pop round to the others who were with us on the skiing trip, and ask them if any of them want to join us. If they do, they'll have to be quick."

Olaf took to Captain Olsen immediately; he looked so dependable.

"Thank God you've come, sir!" he said.

Johan grinned. "You're a bit young to be left in charge of the country's gold reserves, practically on your own. . . . It's not going to be any picnic, you know, getting the stuff out of the country, but we'll collect some reliable men and do the best we can."

Olaf asked the question that was foremost in his mind. "Have you decided how you're going to carry it, sir?"

"In a train."

It sounded so simple that Olaf laughed aloud. "I wish the Finance Minister had thought of that," he said. "Bringing it up in small vans was sheer murder. . . . By the way, sir, could I bring some of my own friends with me on the trip? . . . Three friends?"

"Bring them along to the theatre, and I'll have a look at them."

Johan approached the theatre; it was blacked out, but once inside the atmosphere was convivial. The men were rested and they were keen—he could feel it. He stood for a moment in the doorway, and then one of them suddenly saw him, and sprang to attention. Group after group followed his example, till in a moment everyone was standing up facing him.

"Good evening, gentlemen," he said.

A tall, dignified figure with a huge military moustache detached itself from the others, marched towards him, came smartly to attention and saluted. "Sergeant Borg, sir," he said. "May I help you?"

Johan viewed this apparition—he must be seventy if he was a day; no wonder old Broch had refused to describe him! Still, Johan was getting used to this sort of thing now, and showed no surprise. Apart from his age, the Sergeant presented a very favourable appearance; he was glad he was there.

"Stand the men down, please, Sergeant," he said. "I'd like a brief talk with you."

The order was given in a roar which filled Johan's heart with delight; parade-ground noises of this kind were a part of his life, and somehow this Sergeant made him feel safe again in a world which seemed suddenly to have gone mad. He took him into a small office next to the front door.

"Permanently attached to the Colonel, are you, Sergeant?" he asked.

"Oh, no, sir. I only arrived yesterday; just as well I did. These young devils need watching. They respond quick enough to a sharp order, though; keen as mustard, they are, all of them. Would you care to inspect this batch, sir?"

"Not now," said Johan hastily. "I've called for a very special reason. I'm here to pick a dozen men for an extremely important and secret mission."

Sergeant Borg caught the gleam of excitement in his eyes, and his spirits rose. "You'll be needing a reliable Sergeant with that raggle-taggle bunch," he said at once. "Would you think of taking me, sir?"

"Hadn't you better know what you'd be letting yourself in for before volunteering?"

"Don't you worry about me; I'm as strong as an ox! But if this undertaking is as important as you say, then a good Sergeant is essential."

"Yes, you're quite right. Anyway, this is what it's all about."

He explained as briefly as possible what he had been asked to do, and when he heard himself describing the plan again, it sounded to him even madder than before. However, the old man didn't seem to think so.

"Element of surprise, sir," he said, stolidly. "That's all you need to get the best of Germans. I've fought them before, when I was in the French army. But. . . . " He hesitated. "Only twelve men altogether, sir?"

"Fourteen. Two watches of six each, myself and the driver. The train mustn't attract any attention."

"But as soon as you run into trouble, you'll be bound to lose a few. Then you'll be short."

"True, but I'll be able to replace them from rifle-clubs as I go."

"I suppose so."

"Well, Sergeant, do you still want to join my expedition?"

"Certainly, sir, if you'll take me."

"Right, then," said Johan, "that's settled. Are you able to recommend any of the men out there?"

"A few, yes. But before you choose a crew, you're going to need another officer. You said that the men could be replaced as you go, but that hardly applies to officers."

"A good suggestion, Sergeant, but unfortunately we don't have any!"

"There's a young man here, sir, who's made himself into an officer," said the Sergeant enigmatically. "He's done his military service and two refresher courses, and he's got some men with him."

Johan looked thoughtful. "I'll have a look at him," he said eventually. "You wouldn't have mentioned him if you didn't approve of him, would you?"

The Sergeant's face relaxed. "Only came in yesterday," he said. "He's a good lad—about twenty-seven years old."

"Came in with you, did he?"

"Er—in a way, sir."

Johan smiled. "Well, off you go and get him," he said.
Sergeant Borg went to the door; there was an instant hush.
"Kristian Schwartz!" he bellowed.
A young man came quickly across the hall. "What is it,
Mr Borg?"
"Go to Carl Ringe's house and tell him to come over here
on the double. In his uniform."
Captain Olsen looked quizzically at the Sergeant. "You
know all about this man, don't you?" he said.
"Yes, sir. I'll admit I've known him all his life."
"Trained him, did you?"
"I gave him a bit extra on the side, yes, sir, on top of what
he got in the army. In—in memory of his father. We fought
together in France. We both lived in Lillehammer, and we
used to chat about the old days. And then he died. We both
wanted Carl to go into the army, but he went his own way;
he said promotion was too slow in peace-time."
After a short time, the young man appeared. He was
obviously slightly embarrassed at being faced with a genuine
officer, but he saluted smartly, and waited for the other to
speak first. Johan looked at him for a second, and then suddenly grinned. "Promotion may be slow in peace-time, as you
say, Sergeant," he said, "but even in war time it isn't as fast
as that! Well, how do you do, Captain Ringe."
The boy's expression changed, and one hand went up to
the lapel of his jacket. "I'm terribly sorry, sir," he stammered.
"I told my mother to take off the extra pips before I put on
the uniform; she must have forgotten."
"Whose uniform are you wearing?"
"My father's."
Johan took stock of Ringe; he was well-built and looked
intelligent and reliable. "Commissions in the army aren't
inherited, you know," he said after a while.
"I know that, sir, and I apologize. But, you see, there
weren't any officers here when the war started, so we got out
of town. My men obey me—they are used to taking orders
from me. So if there was any fighting to be done on our own,
it was natural that I should be the leader. And if it came to
being taken prisoner, I'd rather be in uniform than civilian

clothes. I—I'm very glad you've come, sir," he added, and looked as though he really was.

"I've just been sent by General Ruge. I have been asked to carry out a very important and tricky mission, and I've come here to choose a team to help me. Sergeant Borg has volunteered to come with me, and he has recommended you as my second-in-command. I'll tell you all about it in a moment, if you're suitable. But, first, I must ask you a few questions."

It had never been any part of Johan's duties as a training officer to interview men; he started off with what seemed to him a useful question.

"What is your occupation in—er—civilian life?" he asked.

The young man was amused; to the Captain, people obviously fell into two categories—the first, the tiny regular army, and the second, and inferior, category, everybody else. He reminded him of his father.

"I am a skiing instructor, sir," he said.

"Oh?" This had obviously gone down well. "What standard?"

"International."

"And who are these men you've got with you?"

"Four of our best international skiers, Schwartz, Krefting, Eriksen and Astrup. You'll have heard of them, sir."

"Indeed I have," said Johan with interest. "And you planned to join up together, did you?"

"Well, sir, to be honest, not exactly, or we would have been at the front by now. The five of us thought we'd carry out some—er—delaying tactics by ourselves, to harass the enemy. We were practising, so as to be ready for them when they reached Lillehammer, but Mr Borg said every man should join the army. So we came in."

"I see. And just how did you propose to delay the Germans?"

"By killing them, sir," was the simple answer. "But not by shooting them—too noisy. I've taught all my chaps unarmed combat; they're quite good. You see, it's useful for international sportsmen; there are some pretty rough parties after the championships. It's one thing to insure a man, but it doesn't make up to him for being injured, and having to miss events. So we all learnt—just for self-defence, originally."

"Well, well, well!" Johan looked at Borg. "What is your opinion of Ringe's skiers, Sergeant?"

"I can recommend them all, sir."

"Please, sir," begged Carl Ringe. "Tell me what you want us for. It doesn't matter how dangerous it is, you can rely on us."

"Your men have all done their military training? That's essential."

"Yes, sir. All of us."

"Right. Now listen carefully." And he proceeded to explain for a second time that evening the nature of the projected exploit.

Carl's excitement was obvious. Johan was satisfied. "One more point before you bring in your team," he said. "There's no time for proper formalities, so I myself confirm that you hold the rank of acting Second-Lieutenant."

"Thank you, sir. Thank you very much!"

"Off you go, then, and fetch your men in, and don't forget to take off those extra pips. And you, Sergeant, go and hunt up a young man called Olaf Larsen; he'll be in the theatre by now, probably. I promised I'd look at three friends of his. Larsen came up from Oslo with the gold. . . . And look out some more likely lads while you're about it."

A few minutes later, a heated argument came to his ears. He could hear Sergeant Borg's stentorian voice above everyone else's but something was clearly going on over which he had no control. Johan could bellow, too, if the occasion arose. "Sergeant!" he roared. There was instant silence; Sergeant Borg stood to attention, and most of the men.

Johan walked slowly down the steps. "Well, Borg," he inquired, "what seems to be the trouble?"

"Sir, I've found Larsen, but he's got about twelve friends with him, and we only need five more men. And now they've fallen to quarrelling as to who should go."

Olaf Larsen was looking extremely embarrassed.

"Well, Larsen?" inquired Johan.

"Sir, I went to my friends' house, and I was told they were here already—they've been following me!" He scowled at them. "And they've brought a lot of other friends, too. Of course I haven't told them what we're doing, but they seem to have guessed it would be something worthwhile, and now they *all* want to be in on it. Sorry, sir."

"Well, which were the ones you had in mind to start with?"

"Harald, Rolf and Peter Bergstrom, sir. Come here, you lot," he added fiercely, nervous that they might not be accepted after causing such a commotion.

"Can't allow three brothers to serve together," said the Sergeant promptly.

"We were going to join up together anyway," said Harald, "so there's no difference."

"I promised Larsen I'd look at you," said Johan, "and I haven't got all night. So provided you're suitable——"

He gave each of them a sharp glance; they would probably do very well. And then he looked round the ring of eager faces. "We need two more, Larsen," he said. "You know all these men; which would you choose?"

Olaf, feeling all eyes on him, suddenly felt inadequate. "Harald," he whispered, "what do you think? I'd like to suggest Emil Lerdal."

"As you like," said Harald briefly. "And what about Theodor Storm? That makes up the numbers."

"Lerdal and Storm, step forward!" ordered the Sergeant.

Johan looked them both over. "Very well," he said. "Join the others. I'll check you out as quickly as possible."

As they left, there was a despairing cry. "Take *me*, sir——"

"Shut up, you young idiot!" ordered Emil Lerdal. "My brother, Knut, sir," he explained to the captain.

Johan turned and looked at the boy. He hesitated for a moment; but no, he had decided on the numbers. If he wasn't careful he'd land up taking the lot of them. "I'm sorry, boy," he said. "I've got all I need. But stick around; one of these lads may not be satisfactory, and then I'll have a look at you."

When Johan returned to the office with his recruits, he found that Carl Ringe was there already, waiting with his men. When the skiing champions caught sight of Olaf, they all rushed forward to greet him. "Hallo there, Larsen!" cried Astrup gaily. "Where on earth have you sprung fom?"

"I was about to ask you the same question!" cried Olaf. And as his eyes travelled round the room: "Are you all in on this? Good Lord!" and, oblivious of their surroundings, they all burst into loud conversation.

"What the devil——" began Johan.

Carl Ringe took charge. "Attention!" he commanded abruptly. And as the men came immediately to order, he added, "I'm terribly sorry, sir, Olaf Larsen is the junior skiing champion for Norway—we know him very well. We've known him ever since he was paddling round the nursery slopes on baby skis. I'm afraid the surprise made us forget for a moment that we're in the army."

"Some of you are *not* yet," Johan reminded them sharply, and then, seeing the scared expressions, he relented. "I'll overlook your conduct this time," he said. "Sergeant, we seem to be in distinguished company tonight."

"Skiers don't necessarily make soldiers," Borg observed.

Johan glanced at his watch. "Stand these men at ease, Sergeant," he said, "and I'll have a brief talk with each one of them."

He checked them through as well as he could in the time; they seemed a thoroughly good bunch. And then the Sergeant was made to stand at the door to make sure that nobody came in, while he told them what they had been picked for.

"One last and most important question," said Johan finally, "which I'm afraid I forgot to ask the new bunch: have any of you not done your military training?"

The only hand to go up was Olaf's. Johan felt irritated and disappointed: the possibility of Larsen's not having done his training had not even occurred to him. He needed a team that would work well together from the start, which was why he had been anxious to choose men who knew each other, and Olaf Larsen seemed to be the connecting link between them all. How much discipline would a national class skier have, without military training? Probably absolutely none at all. His individual judgement would be sound, but individual judgements made by inexperienced young men on an important mission of this kind were something he felt he could happily do without.

"Why not?" he asked Olaf.

"They couldn't take me! I put my name down, but they didn't have room for me; I was told to go to the university first. But—but my father's taught me how to use a machine-gun. . . . Sir," as an idea struck him, "would you want a spare driver for the train? I know how to drive a steam train; I took my degree in engineering. We did the theory first, and then we were allowed to practise on real trains."

Johan was amused. And relieved. The boy was certainly quick-witted. It had not occurred to him to take a spare driver, but this could just be a face-saver for thêm both.

"Anyone else drive a train?" he asked. There was no answer. "Right, Sergeant; Olaf Larsen, spare train-driver. Stand at ease, and pay attention. . . . You must all realize the tremendous importance of this undertaking, and the need for secrecy. You'll talk to nobody except each other from now on; we'll board the train as soon as everything's ready. In the meantime we must get ourselves organized. I want two watches, one to be Mr Ringe's and one to be Sergeant Borg's. Each watch will have one train-driver, one stoker and one corporal. Larsen, you are Sergeant Borg's driver. As for a corporal for that watch...." He considered for a moment. "Harald Bergstrom," he said, "you will be Sergeant Borg's corporal, and one of your brothers can stoke—see that he learns quickly. Ringe, name a corporal and a stoker from among your men."

"Kristian Schwartz, Corporal," he said, at once. "Ivor Astrup, stoker."

"Very well. And Storm can join your watch, to make your sixth man."

"Sir," Sergeant Borg pointed out, "if Larsen's taking watch and watch with the driver, I'm a man short."

"So you are. . . . Lerdal, has that brother of yours done his military training?"

"Yes, sir, he has."

"Then fetch him in."

As Emil opened the door, Knut practically fell into the room. Red-faced, he stood to attention.

"Sergeant Borg, Knut Lerdal will complete your watch," said Johan. "Explain to him what it's all about."

He stood up. "Now then," he said. "Leave your rifles here, and all of you go across to get your uniforms. N.C.O.s to get stripes. Be back in fifteen minutes, and talk to absolutely nobody on the way."

There was a rush for the door. The Captain glanced at Ringe and Borg. "You two go and check the train," he said briskly. "Let me know how it's getting on."

Carl Ringe soon came back. "Sir," he said, "the train hasn't got moving yet, but they're bringing the gold across pretty fast; it's all in little wooden boxes. I've left Sergeant Borg down there, to make sure that all the stores you ordered are arriving."

"Right. Well, take the men down now to the station-master's office, and keep them there till the train's ready to leave. They're to speak to nobody."

As he went to inspect his train, Johan felt a sudden wild surge of excitement. Supposing they managed it after all? He found Arne Ording at the station talking to Carl Ringe, watching the gold being loaded. There was one truck already covered with tarpaulin sheeting, which Broch told him was to be his home for the next few days; he looked inside. The truck was lighted by a well-shaded lamp, and he saw bedding-rolls, stocks of food and some cooking equipment, plenty of ammunition and the two submachine-guns he had asked for. The machine-guns were on the platform, ready to be mounted at each end of the train among the crates of bullion; white tarpaulin sheeting was waiting to cover each truck as it was loaded, and there was a coal truck.

The driver got out of his cab; he looked a reliable man, and had evidently been told the importance of his cargo. "The loading's gone very well, sir," he said. "It's nearly finished. I shall be glad to get away from here and properly hidden before the morning."

Johan felt suddenly lonely; he was about to set forth into unknown country, with a team of unknown men, beset by dangers which he could only guess at, and yet in charge of the entire gold bullion reserves of his country, without any precise orders as to where to deliver his cargo or when. The snow had stopped, and the sky was clear again; the sickle moon, which had been new on the night of the invasion, was by now giving quite a good light, but the cold, at midnight, was intense. He stood watching with Broch while the final crates were being loaded, and then sent Ringe to fetch his team. Broch wished him good luck, and then they all boarded

the train. Johan told Ringe to take the first watch, and see
that the machine-guns were continuously manned, and then
the train slid unobtrusively out of the station.

About two hours after the departure of the gold train, the
buses which Colonel Broch had sent down to the front full
of reinforcements returned again empty; the convoy woke him
as it trundled to a halt in the square. He went out into the
freezing cold to speak to the drivers; he had not expected
them back again until well after daylight.

The news they brought was ominous: the Norwegian line
was no longer holding. Minnesund had fallen, and General
Ruge was in action with a thousand troops from his training
camp. The German front-line troops had gone to ground for
the night at Minnesund, and Ruge was regrouping the Second
Division a few miles north of the town. Refugees were fleeing
to Hamar; the buses had had difficulty in getting through.
Nervous about the King's safety, Broch woke Ording and told
him the news; they both decided it would be best if he
collected his men and started at once. The shortest route to
Rendal, through Hamar, was still open, but if he waited till
morning he might run straight into a battle for the town, or
be faced with an extremely long drive north round the
mountains. Once at Rendal, he would escort the King north
out of danger, and then west through the only passable valley
to Hjerkinn, where he could allow His Majesty to rest again
while he got in touch with Colonel Hagen at Andalsnes.

After Ording's departure, Broch was extremely busy. He
spent the rest of the day getting all possible volunteers,
uniforms, stores, guns, rifles and ammunition collected together, and then set off for Dombas just as dusk was falling.
Before he left, he told the mayor to take charge of volunteers
who arrived after his departure, and any further supplies of
arms which might arrive, and hold them in readiness as
reinforcements for the Second Division when the retreat
reached Lillehammer.

SIX

"SEARCH THAT TRAIN FOR THE KING"

AS THE GOLD TRAIN gathered speed, the piercing cold penetrated relentlessly through the men's clothing. Johan fell into a light doze, from which he quickly awakened when the train began to slow down. He looked out, and saw to his satisfaction that they had reached Hjerkinn. He went into the cab and asked the driver's advice about a siding. He chose one a long way from the station among some fir-trees, and Johan was content to wait there until it was time for the station staff to come on duty. He hoped to be able to stay for two or three days at Hjerkinn, but after his first discussion with the station-master, it was clear that he would have to think again.

He told him only that he had brought a goods train to Hjerkinn during the night carrying a valuable cargo under army escort, and that he planned to keep it at Hjerkinn at least till nightfall—longer if possible.

"Well, you shouldn't loiter round here too long if your cargo's to be kept out of the hands of the enemy," was the official's discouraging comment. "Where are you heading for?"

"The west coast."

"Hm. Waiting for the allies, I suppose. Well, there's no word of them yet. And the Germans are coming inland from Trondheim; did you know that?"

"I heard, yes. But I don't know how far they've got."

"That's at least one thing I can give you up-to-date information on. I've a brother living a few miles south of Støren, and our plan is that when the enemy gets close he will telephone me, and then drive his family down to me for safety. So I can keep you well posted on that one. Where have you put your train?"

Johan told him, and was just leaving when the telephone

rang. "That might be him now," said the station-master. "You'd better wait a moment and see."

Johan, listening, realized after the first sentence that it could not be his brother—the caller was giving instructions. Finally the official put the receiver down and turned to Johan. "That was from my opposite number at Lillehammer," he said. "Minnesund has fallen, and the Germans are threatening Hamar. I've been told to send no further trains in that direction, but to hold everything here until further orders—not that I've seen any traffic in twenty-four hours! I've got a passenger train waiting at Stören; I'd better bring that down here."

Johan's thoughts went to Otto Ruge, who would now be in the thick of the fighting; if the Finance Minister's message had not come when it did, that's where he would be also. He stood for a moment, lost in thought. "Well," he said eventually, "I'll go back to my train now, and send two soldiers up to the station on duty watch. If you get any fresh news from anywhere, please tell them at once, and one of them can bring it to me immediately."

"Surely. And I'll give you an old railway map, showing all the sidings at every station. Some of them aren't marked on the new maps, because they're disused, but as far as you're concerned they might come in handy."

As he walked back, Johan could hear the men shouting and laughing. The train must on no account attract attention. He called the Sergeant, and told him he wanted to speak to the men. "Tell them to sit down at one end of the truck," he said, "so that I can see them."

After a few moments, he climbed in himself. He sat down on a crate of ammunition, and Carl Ringe and the Sergeant stood behind him. "I want you all to understand right from the start," he said, "that you must make absolutely no noise of any kind. During the day-time, we shall be resting at stations, and we can't have people wandering down to the train to ask what's going on. I don't want to travel in the day-time unless I'm forced to; there are reports of parachute troops dropping at various places, and we've got to avoid them at all costs."

"We'd like to get a crack at them, sir!" called a voice.

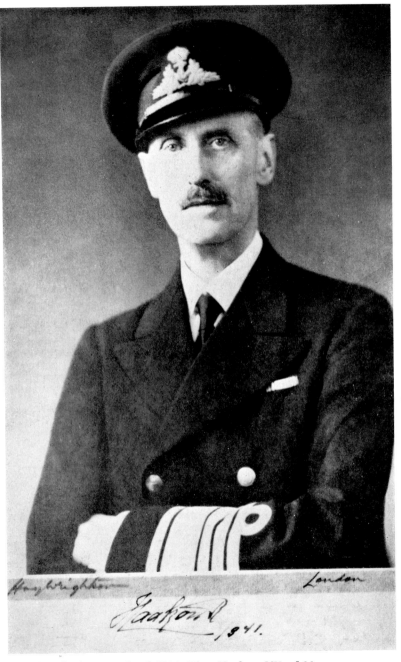

A signed photograph of H.M. King Haakon VII of Norway, 1941,
presented to the author

King Haakon VII of Norway and the Crown Prince Olav, in hiding
in the Gudbrandsdal, April 1940

Eriksen, the Sergeant noticed. "Silence in the ranks!" he roared. "Eriksen, there will be dead silence at all times when an officer is speaking."

The Captain gave Eriksen a sharp glance. "You must all get it out of your heads," he said firmly, "that this is some kind of a sporting event. There will be plenty of fighting, believe me, before this war comes to an end, but this job must be done first. If we are to succeed in getting the gold out of the country, there must be strict military discipline on this train at all times. You will obey orders promptly and efficiently, whether you understand them or not. But we shall *not* deliberately engage the enemy. We have a tremendous responsibility to our cargo, and we shall defend it with our lives if necessary. But, I repeat, we shall fight *only* if there is no alternative. You must understand that if the Germans should be allowed even to become aware of the existence of this train, our chances of success will be practically nil—we will be fifteen men against several thousand. . . . If anyone wants to leave me and go to the front, now is the time to say so."

There was dead silence.

"Well, men?" prompted the Sergeant. "Hands up all those who want to stay with this job and see it through."

Every hand shot up. "All right, then," said the Captain. "But don't any of you forget what I've said. One mistake by one of you could bring the enemy round us like hornets. . . . Astrup and Bergstrom, you are the two stokers; you are to keep the engine ready to leave at any time, and you are responsible for coal and water. Which watch is on duty at the moment?"

"Mine, sir," said Borg.

"Send two of them up to the station. I want a permanent watch kept at every station we stop at; one man on the telephone, one marching up and down outside, changing every twenty minutes. Got it?"

"Yes, sir."

"Larsen!"

"Sir?"

"Get that driver to show you round the engine at once; the sooner you get the hang of the thing, the better. Sergeant,

E

think up some exercises for the men before they freeze. That's all."

Olaf went off to the cab, but the driver said to tell the Guv'nor he was off duty. So he looked round by himself. There was one knob he could see no reason for, and he gave it a tentative press; the result was a loud whistle. The Sergeant appeared at once.

"Cut that out!" he said sharply. "You heard the orders. Where's the driver?"

"He said he wouldn't work during his off-duty time," Olaf told him, "so I came to have a look myself. I didn't like to worry the Guv'nor."

"The *who*?"

"Sorry, Sergeant—I mean Captain Olsen. That was what Bjerkelund called him."

"Who's that?'

"The driver—Jonas Bjerkelund."

"I know his sort," said the Sergeant, "born unco-operative. Still, he's properly within his rights. I'll turn him out as soon as he's had his four hours, and not a moment later. We're not all like that, thank God!"

" 'We', Sergeant?"

Sergeant Borg gave him a conspiratorial wink. "Yes, son, 'we'. I've worked on the railways all my life, except for my nine years in the army. I was a guard for a long time, until I retired eleven years ago."

"But why didn't you mention this to the Captain?"

"He asked if there were any drivers among us," the old man reminded him. "There weren't—although I can actually drive a train; I've done it fairly often. But I'm night-blind now, so I wouldn't be much help, except to advise. But I hope you really can drive. I'm surprised you didn't know that that was the whistle."

"It's a very new model, Sergeant."

"H'm. Get that man to give you a lesson when his rest-time's up."

The fact that the Sergeant could, at a pinch, drive a train took a great weight off Olaf's mind. He had decided privately that Bjerkelund was not a man who would show up well in a crisis, and he was acutely aware of his own inexperience.

If necessary Bjerkelund could be shot, he decided. Arrived at this satisfactory decision he continued to carry out his careful examination of the engine with renewed zest until midday when Jonas Bjerkelund climbed back into the cab, smoking a particularly evil-smelling pipe.

"What are you doing in my cab?"

"Looking at the engine. Will you give me a lesson now, please? I can drive an ordinary engine, so it won't take you long to show me round this one."

"Might as well, I suppose. That old Sergeant of yours woke me up at twelve o'clock on the dot, silly old fool. It's not as if there was any work to be done. . . . Well, I'll show you how she goes, but if you bugger anything up, I'll tan the hide off you!"

Johan and Carl enjoyed a brisk walk through the pine-forest. It was very cold, but the sun shone from a blue sky, and icicles sparkled on the trees.

Johan took the opportunity of explaining exactly what the military picture was just as Ruge had described it to him; there seemed no point in having a second-in-command unless he was in a position to take over at a moment's notice. Also, he gave him the additional news he had managed to glean from the station-master. They decided to walk up to the station before returning to the train, check up on the duty watch and see if there was any more news.

There was. Another call had just come in from Lillehammer. Hamar had fallen, and the Germans were pushing on towards Lillehammer. "Phone back every two hours and ask for news of the German advance," Johan said to the station-master. "I must know exactly where they are."

When the officers returned to the train, they found everything very quiet. There was one piece of news from a different source, which the station-master came down personally to tell the captain: about a hundred parachutists had just been dropped over the Dovre–Dombas area. Some of them had landed in or near Dombas and were being dealt with, but a far greater number had been blown over the thick forests between the two towns, and a good many had come down in Dovre. Every man who could handle a rifle was out after them, and many of them had been shot in the air, but they

had captured the telephone exchange and some adjoining
buildings at Dovre, and it was proving very difficult to dis-
lodge them. Dovre, hardly more than a village, had too few
men to cope.

"They're probably after His Majesty again," said the station-
master. "One can only hope he isn't there."

"He can't possibly be," said Johan briefly. "He couldn't
have got there in the time."

The official would have liked more details, but Johan's
expression discouraged questions.

At dusk the German infantry were reported to have halted
for the night within eight miles of Lillehammer.

It was a difficult decision for Johan. If the enemy were
reinforced during the night, they might well be in a position
to make a big advance during the following day, and he could
find himself being forced to drive by daylight. He would have
to get reliable information somehow during the hours of darkness. Hjerkinn still looked the safest bet at this early stage,
unless news came of the fall of Stören, to the north of him.

Their next contact with the outside world came from a
totally unexpected quarter. At about seven o'clock in the
evening, while Rolf and Emil were on guard duty at the
station, a crowd of people suddenly walked on to the platform, and, head and shoulders above the rest, Rolf recognized
the King. He rushed into the office to tell Emil.

"Perhaps they want to see Captain Olsen," suggested Emil.
"Is Major Ording with them?"

They heard Arne's voice before they saw him. He had gone
straight over to the passenger-train which had recently been
sent down from Stören, and told the driver tersely that his
train was requisitioned, and that he was to go at once to
Lesjaverk. To find a train there at all seemed to him like a
miracle, and this one even had steam up. He had brought the
party to the station on his way west on the off-chance that a
train could be got hold of from somewhere; there were far
too many spotter planes about for his liking, and although the
cars had been camouflaged with lime to make them less
noticeable against the snow they had only been able to make
very slow progress, constantly having to pull off the road and
take cover among the trees. It had occurred to him as he

approached Hjerkinn that if he could get his charge into a train for part of the journey he might be able to put the enemy off the scent.

Rolf and Emil heard him shouting when the station-master had gone across to ask to see his requisition papers. Arne, dead-tired after driving since three o'clock in the morning, told him sharply to stop arguing and take a look at the passengers, and then he could make up his own mind as to their importance. The station-master, recognizing the King and the Crown Prince, immediately hurried over to invite them into his office to get warm while it was being decided what was to be done with the royal cars. Seeing Major Ording alone, Emil and Rolf went over to him and explained who they were. He sent Rolf scurrying down to the train to fetch Captain Olsen, and kept Emil to exchange news.

The train's driver waited about in the background long enough to make sure that his orders were definitely to go to Lesjaverk, and then hurried off to a call-box to telephone his wife and let her know he was coming home. By one of those unfortunate quirks of fate, his home happened to be in Dovre; worried as he was about the safety of his family, the last thing to cross his mind was the possibility that the Dovre telephone exchange might be in the hands of German parachute troops. He merely wanted a few seconds to talk to her—she had been extremely upset when he had phoned that morning from Stören to tell her that he was held up indefinitely, with the enemy only a few miles north of him.

"Darling, this is Rikki," he said as soon as he heard her voice. "I'm at Hjerkinn. I'm going to be able to come home tonight. Once I'm back, I'll stay."

"Oh, Rikki, I'm so glad! I thought you were stuck up north."

"I was, but something's come up. The King's just arrived on the station, with some ministers, and my train's been commandeered. They want to go to Lesjaverk."

"But that's miles from here."

"I know. But they'll have to change trains at the railhead at Dombas—I won't be able to take them any further than that. It's *just* possible that they'll put my train on to the line for the west, if there isn't another, but I can easily get home from Lesjaverk. I must dash now. Good-bye, darling. See you soon."

The German operator who had listened in to this call sent for his Sergeant at once; this was a genuine tip-off, if ever there was one.

"We've got him!" exclaimed the Sergeant. "Well done, lad. Fetch Major Holst at once."

The Norwegian-speaking Major had been dropped with the parachute troops that day with orders to capture the town of Dombas; the information that, owing to an unexpected change in the wind, he had captured key points in Dovre instead, a small town of absolutely no strategic value, had gone down very badly at headquarters. A huge operation was planned for the following day, and no more parachute troops could be spared for a second attempt on Dombas at the moment. Now, however, he would be able to vindicate himself. He got through to the Oslo exchange at once, and asked to speak to Major Lindauer.

"Has the King got any soldiers with him?" he asked gruffly.

"None were mentioned on the telephone, sir. It sounded as though they were trying to pose as ordinary travellers."

"Well, are there any parachute troops at all still in the Dombas area?"

Of those which had landed nearest to the specified target, most were now known to be dead or on their way through the woods to join their companions at Dovre, but it was ascertained by field telephone that a Lieutenant Richter was still within two miles of Dombas, and should have ten men with him. By the time he was contacted, he had already covered another weary mile towards Dovre, and had lost another three men. He was ordered to return immediately to Dombas, go to the station, take it over and look out for a train from Hjerkinn. It had been reported that the King of Norway was travelling on it unguarded on his way to Lesjaverk, and would be obliged to get out at Dombas and change trains for the west. Richter's orders were to take him, preferably alive. The King would probably have to wait on the station for at least twenty minutes, and could not fail to fall into the trap. Lindauer was jubilant; in a few hours' time, Norway would have capitulated.

By the time Richter received these instructions he had already spent some considerable time trudging through the snow in the darkness, in constant danger of being shot by Norwegian snipers. Wearily he and his remaining men turned back towards Dombas, although privately they all thought it extremely unlikely that the King would be within a hundred miles of the place.

Meanwhile, the station-master at Hjerkinn had been making some inquiries of his own, and he quickly discovered that there was no train available to take the King to Lesjaverk from Dombas, nor did he see how this train could be put on to the correct line in the dark without station staff; since no trains were expected, the staff had gone home. He explained all this to Major Ording, warned him about parachute troops at Dovre and Dombas, and suggested that they should take this train straight through to Otta, which was absolutely clear, not stopping anywhere on the way. This plan did, of course, mean driving east towards the advancing Germans, but not very far, and their most important object would have been achieved, which was to shake the enemy off.

Arne glanced anxiously at His Majesty; it was clearly essential that he should be taken somewhere warm, comfortable and comparatively safe at once. After a brief conference, the suggestion was accepted; the chief constable at Otta was to be telephoned and instructed to arrange accommodation for a number of "senior staff officers", who would shortly arrive at Otta station.

Thus by the time the German parachute troops eventually reached Dombas again and took over the deserted station, their royal quarry was safely asleep in a country hotel thirty miles away. Lighting a fire in the office, they took some food and drink out of their packs, and waited patiently for the train to arrive.

Back at Hjerkinn, Johan had gone up to the platform with Rolf as quickly as he could when he got Arne's message, but all he saw was the tail end of the train as it steamed out.

"I'm sorry you missed them, sir," said Emil. "They've just gone to Otta."

"Otta? I thought they were going to Lesjaverk—presumably to join the Cabinet."

"They changed their minds," said Emil. "I don't know why.
Major Ording said to tell you he had decided to take a train
to try to confuse the enemy. He told me to tell you he would
be spending the night at Otta."

Johan, leaving Rolf on the platform, walked slowly back to
his siding. He was puzzled and anxious. In Arne's place, he
could not see himself taking the King down the Gudbrands
Valley towards Lillehammer, but, knowing Arne, he felt sure
he must have had a good reason.

He got his men settled down for the night, but he could
get no rest himself. Threatened from the north and also
possibly from the south, his whole instinct was to get out
under cover of darkness. But where to? He badly needed
up-to-date news—by the time dawn came, it might be too late
to take avoiding action. The Hjerkinn station-master had
promised to let him know what was happening up north. A
call to an official at Stören would only attract attention—a
private call was obviously the safest. He knew nobody at all
who lived in that area. But as to news from the Gudbrands
Valley. . . . And then he thought of Colonel Broch. The old
man would either be still at Lillehammer, and able to supply
accurate information as to the enemy's movements, or else
he would have gone to Dombas with troops as instructed. He
got up at once, told Carl what was in his mind, and walked
up to the station.

He got through to Lillehammer at once; the operator told
him that Colonel Broch had left, and had given instructions
for any calls for him to be put through to the mayor. Having
admitted to the mayor that he was not Major Ording, from
whom the official appeared to be expecting a call, he asked
what time Broch had left town. The mayor was unwilling to
give information to a stranger, but Johan got out of him
what he wanted to know by saying that he was speaking
from General Headquarters. Colonel Broch had left at about
six o'clock, with around 400 men. Putting down the receiver,
he made a rapid calculation. It was about 115 miles from
Lillehammer to Dombas, and Broch should be able to manage
an average speed of 30 miles an hour with troop transports,
so he ought to have reached Dombas at about ten o'clock. It
was now eleven o'clock; if he had arrived in Dombas with all

those soldiers, he would not be difficult to find. Johan picked up the telephone again.

The Dombas exchange confirmed at once that several hundred soldiers had reached the town from the east a short while ago; if Broch was the name of their commanding officer, he thought he should be able to find him fairly easily. Johan settled down to wait.

With his recruits all safely billeted. Colonel Broch was enjoying a pleasant dinner with the mayor, exchanging news and discussing possibilities. He was only waiting to hear that the King had been got to a place of safety, and then he would be able to sleep soundly. As they were drinking their coffee, the telephone rang. The mayor answered it, and said that someone was asking for Colonel Broch, but would not give his name. "Not much escapes our telephone operators," he said. "I certainly didn't tell them myself to put your calls through here!"

Broch was out of his chair and across the room in a moment. "Ording?" he said, hopefully.

But the voice which answered him was the voice of Johan Olsen.

"It's me, sir," he said guardedly. "Do you know who I am?"

"Of course I do. Anything up?"

"Things are getting a bit hot up north," said Johan. "I may have to leave suddenly. Are there any Germans left in Dombas?"

"None," said Broch, promptly. "The ones that were dropped within range of Dombas were counted in the sky, and they have all been dealt with."

The station staff had reported the station clear when they had left at dusk, and in any case the suspicion that some of those in the woods might have doubled back into Dombas had not crossed anyone's mind; Johan would have got an "All Clear" for Dombas whoever he had asked.

"In that case I might come down during the night," said Johan. "But only if I get bad news from the north."

"Very well. You'll be perfectly safe here; I'll call at the station in the morning to see if you've arrived. . . . By the way, I suppose you wouldn't have any news of 'Magnus', would you?"

Johan supposed it could do no harm to use the King's code-name on the telephone.

" 'Magnus' is at Otta," he said.

"What!" Broch was clearly very distressed. "He shouldn't be there, it's not at all safe. A German motorized column has bypassed Lillehammer. The rifle-clubs are busy booby-trapping the road, so none of them will get as far as here, but they could easily reach Otta. Who told you he was there?"

"His new 'nanny'."

There was a pause while Broch worked that one out. Then he said, "What can Ording have been thinking about? He must be got out of there at once."

"It's up to you, then," said Johan. And he hung up before Broch could become more specific. If the Germans didn't know the King was at Otta, they would just drive straight past.

He returned to the train in a much calmer frame of mind. If Dombas was safe, then he had somewhere to run to if there was trouble up north during the night. He told Carl, and immediately fell asleep.

SEVEN

ENCOUNTER WITH PARACHUTE TROOPS

AT ABOUT ONE O'CLOCK in the morning, everyone on the train was awakened by a sharp challenge from one of the guards: "Who's there?"

"It's only the station-master, son," replied a voice. "Can I have a word with the boss?"

The station-master had just had a call from his brother to say that he was coming south at once. German infantry had captured Stören during the night, throwing out what there was of the Fifth Division, who had taken shelter south of the town preparatory to regrouping in the morning. When he had told his wife to get the house ready to receive his brother's family, he remembered the goods train standing in one of his sidings, said to be carrying a valuable cargo; he must go at once and warn the officer in charge to get out of Hjerkinn. He dressed quickly, shivering in the bitter cold, and skied down to the station. The fact that he found himself looking up the barrel of a rifle as soon as he hailed the train told him at once that his journey had been worthwhile; the cargo was obviously extremely valuable.

Johan got to his feet, sleepy and chilly, but by the time the man had finished speaking he was wide awake. "I'll go down to Dombas," he said. "I've been in touch with someone I can trust there, and he said it was quite safe now. How is it for sidings?"

"Got your map?"

Johan took it out of his pocket, and together they studied it by the light of a pencil torch. "Go here," said the station-master after a while. "That siding's buried deep among fir trees, and completely overgrown, but the track's still okay."

As soon as he had gone, Johan said, "Well, you all heard that—we'll leave at once. The engine's stoked, I suppose?"

"Yes, sir," said Astrup. "Ready to start at any time."

"Well, I'm not," came a growl from the floor. "Why can't you wait till the morning, Guv? The Germans won't move till then."

Johan walked across the truck and stood over the driver. "Get up at once," he said sharply. "The train is leaving for Dombas this minute."

"I'm not under military discipline."

"Look here, either you drive, or I'll have you shot; I don't care which. The station-master can get me another driver in ten minutes."

"Okay, okay. Just let me wake up, that's all."

"Larsen," said Johan, "get into the cab with him; watch him carefully, and be prepared to take over."

"This is my train," protested Bjerkelund.

"Only as long as you drive it. Now get along with you, and let's have no more nonsense. Krefting and Eriksen, get into the cab with him as well. Rifles at the ready, and keep your eyes skinned."

Olaf watched Bjerkelund carefully as he got steam up and started to shunt the train back to the platform.

"Why did you make such a fuss?" he asked.

"I don't see so well in the dark. Last night nearly finished me—we get no practice at night, not in goods trains. I thought last night was to be our only night journey, and I wasn't told till the last minute that my own stoker was being left behind; we've worked together for years. But it sounds as if all the driving's to be done at night; I should have been told."

"I see. . . . Well, would you mind if I took over?"

"I'd welcome it. But only if you know what you're doing. If the train goes off the rails, your precious cargo will be dumped for keeps—not to mention the damage you'll do to my train."

"You can watch me."

"You bet I will! If the train's wrecked, I'll lose my job."

Astrup, stoking, overheard this conversation, and passed it on to the Captain; Bjerkelund's attitude was understandable, everyone thought, but without young Larsen they would have been up the creek.

Olaf drove on and on happily into the night, but after some time he began to notice that there seemed to be something

the matter with the brakes, and he said so. Bjerkelund's attitude changed dramatically; it was clear that he had been
paying a good deal more attention to Olaf than it appeared.
He sprang to his feet, knocking the boy out of the way, and
tested the brakes for himself.

"It's your bloody cargo—that's what's the matter with the
brakes. It's too heavy. The air-brake on one of the trucks
must have worked loose; it's lucky it hasn't come adrift altogether. We could all get killed. I should have had more warning before loading up with this type of thing. Anyway, we're
just running into Dombas. I'll take her in; you keep out of my
way. As soon as we've put her to bed, I'll test the brakes.
You can help me. Go and ask the Guv'nor where he wants
her put, and come back and tell me."

Olaf got the necessary information, and went back to the
cab. It was now about two o'clock in the morning. Both
watches were on the alert as the train slowed down at
Dombas station, and the machine-gunners were quickly sent
to their posts; Johan was taking no chances. He himself was
looking out between the top of the truck and the tarpaulin.
As the train went past the platform, he tensed; he could have
sworn he had seen what he most dreaded to see—the glint
of moonlight on a steel helmet. But he had been assured that
Dombas was clear. . . . He touched Sergeant Borg's arm and
pointed urgently; the one he had seen had disappeared in the
gloom, but they were now just passing another. Lieutenant
Richter and his paratroopers had heard the sound of the
train's approach a few minutes earlier; after waiting for
several hours for a train reported to be carrying the King of
Norway, Richter had been on the point of telephoning to
Dovre for permission to rejoin their unit, but now that they
could hear a train actually approaching their dejection
vanished. The Norwegian King was coming that way after all.

They were puzzled that the train did not stop at the station,
and disconcerted when it was seen to be a goods train. Their
old doubts began to return.

"Dear God!" murmured Rudolf Borg. "It's unbelievable!
Surely they can't have forgotten to check the station?"

"Lerdal, cut across to the driver," whispered Johan, "and
tell him he's not to stop; he's to go straight on to Rauma."

Emil vanished, and the Bergstrom twins went over to the Captain. "What's up, sir?" they asked apprehensively.

"Germans."

"But we were *told*——"

"I know, I know. Anyway, if we can get to the next station we might be able to hole up there instead."

As he spoke the train came to a halt, some distance past the platform, and Emil Lerdal reappeared. "Bjerkelund says we can't go to Rauma, sir—not at the moment, that is. We're on the Hjerkinn—Dombas—Lillehammer circuit. He'll have to get her on to the western line, and that means waiting till dawn."

"Till *dawn*? Bring him here at once, and Larsen and the guards."

When Bjerkelund arrived, he looked nervous.

"Get the train on to the Lesjaverk line at once," whispered Johan, urgently.

"I *can't*, Guv. With no lights and no station staff, it's not worth risking. We'd derail the train for sure."

"I see. . . ." So that, Johan realized at once, was why Arne had been obliged to take the King back to Otta. . . . "Well, I suppose we'll have to accept that. In which case, we'd better take a little trip up to the station; it appears to be in the hands of the Germans. We'll see how many there are. We might be able to—er—eliminate them."

"Good idea, sir!" agreed Carl enthusiastically. "We could get some German helmets. They might come in very useful later on if we run into any more of them!"

"If you're thinking of fighting," said Bjerkelund quickly, "you can put that idea right out of your heads. There'll be no fighting on my train."

"What the hell d'you mean?"

Olaf's temporary sympathy for Bjerkelund evaporated immediately. "He's probably calculated that he's off duty," he said contemptuously, "but he's not—not till three o'clock."

"It's my watch all right, but it's not my fight! Look here, Guv'nor, I should have told you this before—I'm a neutral. I'm Swedish, and the train, she's Swedish too; so fighting's not on."

There was a silence. Nobody was to blame for not guessing;

anyone living near the long border between the two countries might easily speak with a Swedish accent. Suddenly everyone started talking at once.

"Shut your noise!" ordered Sergeant Borg in a reverberating whisper. "The Germans will hear you, you stupid bastards! . . . Sir, I say we ought to ditch him; neutrals are worse than the enemy. You can't tell which way they'll jump."

"We can't 'ditch' the driver, Sergeant!" said Johan. "Bjerkelund, why did you offer to do this job at all?"

"For money, sir. The station-master at Lillehammer said I'd be well paid. You see, I'd been stranded at Lillehammer since the Germans walked into Norway—I telephoned Head Office in Stockholm, and they told me to do what I thought best. The station-master said this job was urgent, so we threw out the junk I had on board and took on you and the gold instead. I understood it was just to be a direct trip to the west coast."

"You saw the machine-guns being mounted."

"I thought they were for self-defence."

"So they are. We expect to be attacked."

"The trip's worth a lot of money, Guv'nor."

Johan regarded him with distaste. "It looks as though we're stuck with you," he said. "But if it's money you're after, you can earn some right now. Have you got your passport?"

"Yes, sir, of course."

"What's written on the train's consignment papers?"

"Spare parts for cars."

"Let's have a look." Johan crossed out the original words, leaving them clearly legible, and wrote "ammunition" over the top, and gave the papers back to Bjerkelund. "Now, listen to me," he said, "this is what you're to do. When the Germans come sniffing round this train, as they're bound to do sooner or later, you're to tell them it's a Swedish train that's been commandeered by their own people at Lillehammer, to take ammunition to the German army to form a secret dump for them somewhere near the west coast. If you succeed in deceiving them, you'll get 200 kroner now, and more later. But if you try to double-cross us, we'll shoot you. Is that clear?"

"Quite clear. But I'm not sure I can act that well."

"Not much need for acting at all," said Johan briefly. "Just

show them your papers if they ask, and look annoyed if they
ask too many questions. Off you go now, back to your engine.
They'll probably be here soon. And while you're talking to
them, remember that there are two machine-guns trained on
you. . . . Ringe, go and tell your machine-gunners not to fire
unless they're told."

After a few minutes Sergeant Borg, who had been fixedly
watching the station, turned round. "I think they're coming
now, sir."

"Larsen, go and tell Bjerkelund to look alive."

Shortly, they heard the ring of boots on the platform in
the distance, and, by the light of a rapidly approaching lantern,
they could see a German officer and two soldiers.

"They'll be cold," said Johan quietly. "If they believe
Bjerkelund—and he can show them the train's papers and his
passport—they'll probably go straight back to the warmth.
But there won't be just the three of them, you can be sure of
that; there'll be men behind them in the dark keeping them
covered in case of trouble—how many is anyone's guess."

The three Germans passed within six inches of the watchers;
they went straight to the driver's cab, and their conversation,
in German, was clearly audible, and understood easily by the
crew. Bjerkelund was gruff, but he was convincing.

Not only a goods train, but Swedish, eh? Lieutenant Richter
realized it was extremely unlikely to be carrying the royal
party, and he felt irritated and disappointed. Another bloody
rumour, just as he had suspected, and they could have been
safely in Dovre by now, warm and comfortable with the rest
of the lads. That Dovre would now be in German hands he
had no doubt at all; he knew there were no Norwegian soldiers
there. However, he persisted in his questions, because if he
had not done so his Sergeant, who was a Nazi, would have
spread it about that he had been slack. The Sergeant peered
under one or two of the tarpaulins, and saw nothing but piles
of wooden boxes. The light had been put out in the sleeping-
quarters; he did not approach that particular truck—if he had
done so, he and the rest of them would have died instantly.

"Where did you say this ammunition was being taken to?"
asked the Sergeant.

General Otto Ruge,
Commander-in-Chief
of the Norwegian
Army

General Carl Fleischer,
Commander of the
Sixth Division, North
Norway, and after the
surrender Comman-
der-in-Chief of the
Norwegian Army (in
exile)

Captain Johan Olsen (*left*) (a photograph taken in London in 1941, in British khaki). (*right*) Colonel O.-J. Broch (the author's cousin) in 1941

Extreme right, back row, of this group is Harald Bergstrom, 'somewhere in England'. in training, 1941

"I didn't," replied Bjerkelund rudely. "I said 'somewhere secret near the west coast'. And I meant it."

"We were told you might have the King on board this train," said Richter.

The remark took Bjerkelund completely by surprise. "The King?" he exclaimed. "What king, may I ask?"

His astonishment was so obviously genuine that Richter felt a little foolish. "The King of Norway," he replied sharply.

Bjerkelund laughed. "You're barmy! Whoever heard of carrying a king in a goods train? Anyway, the last I heard of him he was near the Swedish border—probably gone over there by now, I shouldn't wonder. Wish I was there, too."

Although Richter disliked being made to look foolish, particularly in front of his men, there were still one or two more questions he had been told to ask.

"Is your name Rikki?" he said next.

"Look here, Guv'nor, are you drunk or something? My name's Jonas Bjerkelund—you've seen it on my passport. Try and make 'Rikki' out of that."

"Well, have you got a wife in Dovre?"

"No I have not! My wife's in Sweden."

"Girl-friend, then?"

By now Bjerkelund was really angry. "Damn you!" he exploded. "Will you get off my back? Perhaps you'd like to tell me what you're doing on Dombas station? I don't think you're looking for any king; it looks to me as though you'd just dropped in here to get away from the fighting for a while."

"Speak respectfully when you address a German officer," ordered the Sergeant sharply.

"I might if he asked sensible questions. What's eating you, Guv.? You know you're not supposed to plague neutrals."

Richter didn't in the least mind plaguing neutrals in the ordinary way, but the Swedes were pro-German neutrals, which was what this impudent lout was hinting at. "No more questions," he said. "It's just that we have orders to intercept a train coming through here carrying the King of Norway and some officials of the Norwegian Government."

"Well, you'd better wait for them, hadn't you?" said Bjerkelund cheekily.

F

As they turned to go, Bjerkelund was struck by what he considered a brainwave; the Captain wanted to go west—he couldn't be discovered here by the enemy in the morning. These Germans could help him to move the train. "Sir," he said, "could you lend me your men and the lantern to put this train on to the right line for the west?"

"Take the lantern, Sergeant," said Richter, "and get that train on to the right track; I'll go back to the office."

Bjerkelund and the German Sergeant glared at each other. "Come on, sunshine," said Bjerkelund. "You heard what the man said. Do as I tell you, and it won't take long. You can move the points with the hand-levers, and mind you move them the whole way across, or you'll derail the train, and then what's left of you won't be worth looking at when they drag you out from underneath."

The Sergeant made a signal, and five more soldiers, who had been surrounding the train in the darkness, joined him. Johan hoped that was the lot. In half an hour the train was moved, and then they started walking up and down it, making clanking noises. "What are they doing?" Johan whispered to Olaf.

"Testing the brakes. I told Bjerkelund something was wrong. He thinks it's one of the air-brakes, due to the weight of the cargo."

"I hope he puts it right."

"We'll have to keep testing, all the time."

Johan nodded. Then the freezing soldiers started to go back to the platform, and everybody began to relax; Bjerkelund seemed to have really earned his money. Just as Johan was about to go and congratulate him, the soldiers stopped and shouted—they were inviting the driver to come back with them for a drink. He thanked them, but said he did not like to leave an ammunition train unguarded. But by this time, the train was much nearer the platform, and the Sergeant insisted. He seemed to have taken quite a liking to Bjerkelund; perhaps he found his impertinence amusing.

"The train's all right—we can see it from here," he said. "I've never met a Swede who refused a drink."

So Bjerkelund accepted the invitation; there was really no alternative, without arousing suspicion. The Norwegians glanced at each other; they would all have to keep alert, and the machine-guns would have to be continuously manned. A Swedish driver drinking spirits with the enemy not a hundred yards away was a very tricky position to be in.

It did not take Bjerkelund long to get thoroughly drunk; he came staggering out, supported by the German Sergeant, and groped his way back to the cab. He had an arm round the German's neck, and he was whispering in his ear and laughing. It was obvious that the Sergeant most certainly was not drunk, and was paying careful attention to what the Swede was saying. He practically threw Bjerkelund back into the cab, and then gave a shout. "Sir," he called, "would you please come and examine this cargo?"

Richter was standing in the doorway. "What for?"

"That clown says he's carrying gold bullion."

The Lieutenant laughed. "No need to pay any attention to that," he called back. "He was just trying to make himself important. He's drunk, remember."

"Nevertheless, it wouldn't take long to make sure." Baulked of his prey, the Sergeant felt that gold bullion might be a reasonable substitute.

"Please yourself, then," replied the Lieutenant, "but don't blame me if you freeze to death."

The man climbed up on to one of the trucks and removed the tarpaulin. He stared thoughtfully at the wooden crates; they were unmarked. Suddenly he straightened up; he had evidently come to a decision. He jumped down, went back to the waiting-room, and reappeared with three more soldiers.

"They're coming to examine the cargo," said Johan. "Ringe, you'll have to tell your forward gunner to open up on them as soon as they come within range. Bjerkelund's blown the gaff, so we've no longer got any choice."

"You mean—you mean just mow them down, sir?"

"Well, what the devil do you want to do? Ask them to tea? You were keen enough on getting German helmets half an hour ago."

"Yes, sir, I still am. But a machine-gun——"

"Is unsporting? War isn't sporting, boy. It isn't a game."

He understood Carl's feelings perfectly. To kill for the first time in cold blood was a difficult thing for anyone to do, particularly with a machine-gun—this was where field experience came in. But Johan had no intention of evening up the odds.

The Germans were still chatting in the doorway; he had his eye on them. "Well, Ringe," he said, crisply, "you heard my order."

"It's them or us," interrupted Olaf Larsen, suddenly. "They started it. They came here, dropping bombs everywhere. It's their fault. Think of them as vermin."

Johan glanced at Carl Ringe, who was still hesitating. "You may recall your gunner, if you can't trust him to do his duty," he said. "I have a better man here beside me."

Carl's head went up. "Eriksen will obey an order!"

"So give Eriksen the order, Ringe," snapped Johan.

He put his hand on the young man's shoulder. "It's not only 'them or us'," he said, urgently. "It's them or the King! He *did* go through here a few hours ago, on his way to Otta; their information service must be pretty good. So see that they're destroyed, before they catch him."

To his satisfaction, Carl Ringe's hesitation seemed to disappear.

Rudolf Borg breathed a sigh of relief; he had feared that his protégé was going to fall at the first fence. He looked back again towards the station, and then touched the Captain's arm.

"Sir," he whispered. "I've had my eye on their officer for some time—I can just see him through the doorway, and he's standing under the light. I thought he was talking to someone who was out of sight, but he isn't; he's on the bleeding telephone."

"He must have decided to take Bjerkelund seriously after all, and is making a report," said Johan. "We'd better put an end to his conversation at once. Here's where I get my own German uniform! Larsen, lend me your rifle; he's a bit far away for a certain shot with a pistol."

Johan moved across to where Borg had been standing, took careful aim and fired; they all saw the officer fall forward. After a split second of sheer amazement, the German soldiers leapt into action. One immediately turned out the light, and taking advantage of the fact that the sniper would require a short time to accustom his eyes to the sudden darkness, they made a concerted rush towards the train. They were making straight for the cab; it was clear from this that Bjerkelund had not mentioned the train's crew, but only its cargo. They obviously thought that they had only one drunk civilian to deal with, and therefore were not taking any precautions. A hundred yards separated them from the train, and they had not gone half the distance when everyone's eyes had recovered, and they could see the dark uniforms of the advancing figures clearly against the snow.

Johan handed Olaf back his rifle, reloaded. "If the machine-gunner doesn't shoot," he said, "we'll kill them ourselves before they reach us."

But as it happened his precautions were unnecessary. Eriksen, who had been watching everything, had expected to be told to fire, and his machine-gun was already bearing on the enemy when Carl reached him. As its murderous chatter began, a shower of snow was thrown up behind the running soldiers. He closed the range, and in another three seconds all four were lying dead in the snow. Rolf Bergstrom sat down rather suddenly on a pile of bedding, and Peter also felt sick. No one spoke, and then they heard Carl Ringe returning. "Dead on the nail, sir!" he announced proudly. "What about the rest?"

Even Johan was amazed at the transformation; in the past few minutes, Carl Ringe had become a soldier. "Well, what was your original plan for getting a steel helmet, Carl?" he asked.

"To creep round and take them unawares, sir."

Johan gave a laugh of genuine amusement. "There's no chance of that now!" he said. "That machine-gun made the devil of a row. If there are any Germans this side of Dombas, they'll be descending on us like a cloud of locusts! . . . But apart from that, there should be three more actually on the station. We'll have to flush them out somehow, or we'll never get any sleep. . . . Yes, Bergstrom, what is it?"

Rolf was still sitting on the floor, and he had plucked the tail of Johan's greatcoat sharply. "Sir," he whispered, "there's something going on under the train."

"What, boy?"

"I can hear people talking."

A tap on the Sergeant's arm, and they had both joined Rolf on the floor, listening. They stood up, and conversation in the truck ceased.

"Carry on talking," said Johan hastily. "At least two of them are under the train—possibly all three. Act quite normally, while I decide what to do."

After a moment's thought, he looked up. "We'll try an old trick on them," he said. "One man will lower a flashlamp on a cord at the rear of the train to attract their attention, and another man with a tommy-gun will go down on to the coupling between the front truck and the engine. The enemy will look towards the light at once and shoot at it; at the same time, it will illuminate them, which should give the man with the tommy-gun a chance to catch sight of them just before the light's shot out, and get them from behind . . . Keep talking! . . . Corporal Schwartz, take Astrup with you, and cover for him while he goes down on to the front coupling. You should each have a submachine-gun. . . . Where the hell are the damned things?"

"Here, sir," whispered Astrup. "I've got them both. Come on, Kristian."

"Wait!" said Johan. He bent down. "Are they still there, Bergstrom?" he asked Rolf softly.

"Yes, sir. But they're no longer under our truck. They've moved—they're one along, towards the end. Somebody just sneezed."

Johan straightened. "Krefting, you can climb along the top of the trucks and lower the lighted torch at the far end of the train," he said, "but the gunners will have to know exactly when you've got there. Have we any cord?"

"Only what the bedding rolls are tied together with," said someone.

"Some of you men, cut off all the cord you can find and knot it quickly together," said the Captain. "Astrup and Krefting will each hold one end of the cord. When Krefting is in position at the far end of the train, he is to give two sharp tugs, and then switch on the torch and lower it. That should give Astrup a second or two to get into position and start firing, while the enemy turns to face the light. Has anyone got a torch?"

"Here you are, sir," said Borg. "I've tied a piece of string on to its ring, so that it can be lowered."

Peter, Rolf and Olaf rapidly cut the cords from the bedding rolls with their pocket-knives, and tied them all together into one long piece. "That's all there is, sir," said Olaf. "It looks enough."

"Right. Krefting, take one end of the cord, and off you go. Astrup, keep a tight hold of the other end, and you and Schwartz stand by to cut down on to the front coupling as soon as Krefting lets you know he's ready with his torch."

As the three of them vanished, Johan noticed that the rest of the men were still talking as ordered; Sergeant Borg was making sure of that.

Suddenly they heard the sharp chatter of Astrup's machine-gun and then there was a loud shout from Schwartz: "You damned idiot, don't go after him! . . . Sir, there's a man cutting out from under the train on the platform side. Can you get him?"

Johan caught a glimpse of the dark, moving shape, fired once, and it fell.

"Another torch, please, sir!" called Schwartz. One was immediately passed to him, and he shone it under the truck. No one left, as he had thought. He went back with Astrup to make his report, and Krefting climbed thankfully back to the comparative warmth of the truck. There had been three soldiers under the train, which meant that all the ones they had actually seen had been accounted for, but there was still the danger that more might be lurking somewhere about. "Sergeant," said Johan, "before we turn the light on, I'd like you to take two men and check whether the station's clear. All wear your white coats and hoods, and get off the train at the rear. Keep flat and keep in the shadows; get on to the platform from the far end, and cut in through the goods shed."

The Sergeant's old bones creaked as he crawled about, but he did not mind. He was happy just to be back in action again, as he had never expected to be, and serving with Björn Ringe's son. The fact that he had been sent at all was another source of satisfaction; to him it meant that the Captain considered him expendable, which in turn could only indicate that young Ringe, in the Captain's eyes, had come satisfactorily through his baptism of fire.

There was absolutely no one on the station; when the three of them returned to say so, Johan sent four men to fetch all the German overcoats and helmets, and the officer's cap and overcoat for himself, and told them to drag the corpses out of sight. He decided that, at least until they left Dombas, the duty watch should wear German uniform, just in case the enemy was keeping the station under observation. If this lot could arrive without anyone in Dombas knowing anything about it, there was nothing to prevent others. The overcoats and headgear only were necessary, since the uniform of both armies, except for minor details, was exactly the same. When the men returned, they said it was as well the captain had not wanted the uniforms, as they were already frozen stiff to the corpses. Johan would have to test his team's German in the morning, so as to be sure they could answer convincingly if challenged, but he hadn't any real doubts on this score: all Norwegians were taught German at school, to a high standard.

It was time to relax and have a meal. Someone suddenly remembered Bjerkelund, who was still in his cab, and brought him in, fast asleep and snoring. "It's a good thing he's asleep," said Johan, "or he'd hear what we're saying about him. Christ, what a cock-up!"

"He gave us a chance to have a crack at them, sir!" said Eriksen cheerfully.

"What I'm worried about is what their officer said on the telephone, and to whom."

"I expect we'll know soon."

"Undoubtedly! . . . We'd better all get as much rest as possible, so as to be ready to deal with them if they send anyone over here."

EIGHT

OUTWITTING THE GESTAPO

JUST AFTER EIGHT O'CLOCK, Johan was awakened from a light sleep by a touch on the shoulder. He reacted violently at first to the sight of a German soldier bending over him, and Kristian Schwartz sprang out of his way. "Sorry!" he said. "It was that uniform—I nearly killed you."

"Not a chance!" contradicted Schwartz, in an amused voice, and then added, as an afterthought, "Sir."

"You lot are dangerous," said Johan, grinning. "I begin to wish I hadn't brought you! Is anything wrong?"

"I'm not sure, but there may be. Mr Ringe sent me. One of their spotter planes has been circling over the station. As soon as we heard it, Ringe told Krefting and Eriksen to start marching up and down the platform, and when it flew over the pilot couldn't have helped seeing them, and might have been reassured by the sight of German uniforms. But of course one can't be sure. Carl wondered whether we ought to move on at once."

Johan considered. "Moving on wouldn't help," he said eventually. "Nothing's easier to spot from the air than a train—even at night, if it's under observation. We'll wait to see whether they decide to take another look at us. If they do, it'll mean they aren't satisfied. How they'll act then remains to be seen. If we can't shake them off we might—er —just be out of luck."

"You mean they'd follow us wherever we went?"

"Wherever we went *in this train*. But the very thought of lorries. . . . Well, it's no use losing heart yet. Everything really depends on what their officer said on the telephone last night. Tell Ringe there's no point in getting into a flap yet; just bring me some coffee—I can smell it."

A few moments later, Carl Ringe came on board, wearing the German officer's cap and overcoat. "Christ almighty!"

exploded Johan. "I wish you'd give some kind of warning before you appear in that uniform!"

Carl glanced round the truck and saw that the off-duty watch, who had been wakened when Schwartz came in, had all instinctively reached for their rifles. "Sorry, sir," he said. "I'll have myself formally announced next time I'm coming on board! . . . Schwartz says you've decided to stay here."

"For the moment, yes. We'll see if they make any further moves. And Colonel Broch said he'd call this morning; the British might have landed by now—they've had time—and he'll know about that."

Exactly an hour later, Olaf's sharp ears caught the sound of a plane's engines, and he called out to the Captain. "Give me the German cap and overcoat, Ringe," he said at once. "I'm going on to the station."

Johan was standing at the door of the station-master's office by the time the plane came into sight, a small reconnaissance plane flying very low. He took two steps forward smartly, came to attention, and raised his right arm in the Nazi salute. The plane, now directly overhead, dipped a wing, and then completed its circle and vanished in the direction of Oslo.

"So far, so good," commented Johan. "I just had a hunch that they might want confirmation that everything was in order, and I guessed the sight of an officer might reassure them. They seem to be making hourly checks, so if they don't come back by ten o'clock or thereabouts, we might reckon we're in the clear. Then I'll get in touch with Andalsnes and see if they're ready for us yet. It's only fifty miles."

At ten o'clock precisely the plane was back again, and Johan went through the same performance again, and received the same acknowledgement to his salute. "Ringe," he said, when he got back to the team, "I don't like it. Next time they might flash a signal, and then we'll be in real trouble, because we won't be able to decode it."

"We could make a note of it, sir," said Carl hopefully. "Maybe someone at Andalsnes will have broken the German code by now."

The possibility that the Norwegians might have broken the German code in one week was in the highest degree unlikely; he assumed that Carl had made the remark in order to try to reassure the men. They had been told that the German army was advancing on Dombas from two directions—how close the enemy was by now was anybody's guess, and to be stuck at Dombas itself was suicidal. They would have to move, and soon, even if it meant driving nonstop to Andalsnes. At least the Fourth Division was there—what there was of it.

"If Colonel Broch doesn't call soon, I'll try to get him on the telephone. Some fresh information would be a help," Johan said.

He decided to walk over to the station-master's office where the duty-watch had made a fire of sorts, and have a quiet smoke on his own while he tried to work out his problem. But before leaving he told Carl to make sure that all the men could speak good German.

"We speak it like natives," Carl told him, "as we are so often in Austria and Switzerland, but I'll ask the others."

The men immediately appreciated the significance of the question. It appeared that the younger ones spoke German fluently; only Harald Bergstrom and Theodor Storm were a bit rusty, though they understood it perfectly. Johan told them that, if challenged, they had better be Bavarians. Johan's own German was excellent, and Rudolf Borg also appeared to be a good linguist, speaking excellent French as well.

Two of the men were marching up and down the platform in steel helmets, rifles at the slope, and the plane wouldn't be back for nearly an hour, if it kept to its present schedule; Johan reckoned he would have made up his mind what course of action to take by then.

As he crossed the platform, a familiar voice shouted urgently, "Johan, what the devil are you playing at? You nearly gave me a heart-attack!"

"Sorry, Arne, truly," he replied, as Arne Ording strode on to the platform, accompanied by a very nervous-looking signal-man. "But I'm in the devil of a mess. . . . I'm glad to see you; I was expecting Colonel Broch. Have you brought the King to Dombas?"

"Yes. We got here in the middle of the night; Broch organized it. I gather he was acting on information from you. He's asleep at the moment, worn out, so I came to see you instead. . . . But before we say any more, you must put guards on the station *at once* in Norwegian uniforms, or you'll all be shot. The town's swarming with troops, British, French, Poles and God knows what else—about 800 of them. The first troopship arrived at Andalsnes last night, and they've been sent by road straight to Dombas. And just in time. You'd better put someone on duty as quickly as you can."

Johan called one of the station-watch, and told him to fetch Mr Ringe at once.

"Do I take it that everything's in order, then?" asked the signalman.

"It is, thank God," said Arne. "So you can fetch the station-master; Captain Olsen might need him. . . . When I walked up to the station," he went on, when the man had left, "I noticed that fellow cowering behind a shed. He was just coming on duty, and saw the uniforms. He warned me, and when I'd crouched down beside him for a while I thought I recognized some of the men's faces, and then I saw you. It was a very nasty moment!"

Carl Ringe then appeared with several men, anxious to hear at first hand any news Major Ording might have brought, and the news of the allied landing was greeted with loud cheers. "But only one ship?" asked someone.

"So far. But more are on their way, they say."

Carl was told to put men in Norwegian uniforms at every access point to the station, and then Arne insisted on being told immediately what was going on. Johan described their adventure of the previous night, and how his decision that the station-watch should wear German uniform had been proved to be justified by the unwelcome attentions of the spotter plane that morning.

Arne was alarmed. "You're certainly in trouble," he said. "If you wear Norwegian uniform, the enemy will probably send down paratroopers ahead of you and block the line, and if you wear German uniform you're likely to be shot by us or the allies. You say the plane comes over every hour?"

"That's what it's been doing so far, yes."

"Well, you'll just have to make a lightning dash away from Dombas between visits."

"That's the only thing I *can* do. . . . I wonder if you'd do something for me. Could you tell the exchange to warn the rifle-clubs along the line as far as Lesjaverk to be on the look-out to protect us from stray paratroopers, and tell them we'll be in German uniform—it's safer, in case that plane decides to escort me. If it does, I'll make a dive for cover the minute it's out of sight—anywhere. After what happened here yesterday, the exchange would probably think we really *were* Germans, if I telephoned them from here! If I can be sure you've done that for me, I'll leave directly after my friend's next visit. And I'll just have to hope it won't signal instructions to me when it comes. If instructions come in code, I'll have to ignore them."

"As long as you acknowledge them, that's all that matters. Then go hell-for-leather along the Lesjaverk line, and find a good hideout. . . . Christ, what bad luck! Is your Swedish driver pro-German?"

"Not noticeably; he just wants money. He'll stick on our side as long as he thinks there's cash in it. . . . Before you go, Arne, tell me what happened to you last night."

"Well, as soon as Broch had spoken to you, he telephoned the chief constable at Otta and asked for me by name, so nothing was given away over the phone. When we heard that a German motorized column had bypassed Lillehammer, we decided we would have to move at once—Otta's only 80 miles further up the valley. They were busy booby-trapping the road all the way along in front of the Germans, and as soon as we got a message back to Headquarters that we were at Otta they left the 35 miles from Otta to Dombas clear for us—it'll all be booby-trapped by now. The only awkward place to get through was Dovre; the Germans are still holding parts of it, and they've got the telephone exchange. So Broch charged down to Dovre with about 200 volunteers to see us through. Luckily they were all in uniform, so the enemy were deceived into thinking they were soldiers; I gathered that most of them had had no training at all! But they let off their pop-guns in all directions, and in the confusion we managed to drive past. The Germans stayed firmly inside the buildings they had occupied, and fired from there, which made them fairly easy to avoid."

"It must have been quite a night."

"It was. Christ, I'm tired! I've got to let them all rest for

a while—we want to get the King to England alive, not dead!
—and then we're going straight to Lesjaverk to join the other
ministers. From there they can get in touch with Andalsnes
on the telephone. . . . This first contingent of allied troops will
help morale a lot. Half of them are to wait here to engage
whatever units of the German army get past the obstacle-race
that's been prepared for them, and the other half have departed towards Stören, to back up the Fifth Division. The
Germans, I hear, are retreating on that front already, because
they're in danger of being cut off from their base; the British
Navy have been attacking Trondheim."

Sergeant Borg appeared then in the doorway. "That plane's
coming back again sir," he announced.

"Very well. Excuse me a minute, Arne, will you? Just
watch this."

Arne watched the ceremony with some amusement, and
was relieved to see that, apart from dipping a wing in salute,
the plane did not signal.

"You see what I mean?" said Johan, as he returned to the
office. "He's got me cornered! If only I had one little anti-
aircraft gun——"

"Yes, I know how you feel. Well, I'll be off now and get
the clubs warned for you, so that you can get moving at
once."

"Thanks. My respects to His Majesty."

"Of course."

Johan was a great deal more worried than he cared to
admit to his crew. There were no more trains running now,
and the enemy had complete command of the air. His one
comfort was that the Germans would use neither bombs nor
machine-guns on him—they wanted the gold intact, and they
would need the train to carry it in.

After Arne's departure, Johan gave the German officer's
cap and overcoat back to Carl Ringe and told him to walk
about on the station for a while wearing it, just in case the
plane should alter its routine, while he went to explain the
exact position to the men, and tell them to have the train
ready to leave Dombas at once.

Carl looked inside the cap. "Hans-Wilhelm Richter," he
read aloud, "from Heidelberg."

As Johan was returning to the train the telephone rang, and the station-master, who had arrived a few minutes before with the signalman, picked up the receiver.

"*Ja?*" he said, and then nearly dropped the instrument in his astonishment. Recovering himself, he placed it gently on the table, and tiptoed across to Carl Ringe. "There's a German officer from Dovre asking to speak to Lieutenant Richter," he whispered, "and since that appears to be his cap you're wearing——"

"Christ, are you sure?"

"I'm sure. It's a good line. What the hell are you going to do? If someone doesn't speak to him, they'll get suspicious and fly in some more parachutists."

"I'll fetch Captain Olsen. . . . You only said '*Ja*' on the telephone, didn't you?"

"That was all."

"Well, that's the same in German, fortunately. . . ."

Carl picked up the receiver and said "*Ein Moment,*" put it down again, and then started to run after Johan, only remembering just in time that German officers didn't run—they strutted. For the benefit of the German caller, he yelled: "Herr Leutnant! Telefon!"

Johan looked round in surprise, and Carl beckoned to him urgently; when he was close enough to hear a whisper, Carl was able to explain his strange behaviour.

"A German officer speaking from Dovre, eh?" exclaimed Johan. "We'll get some orders at last, and then we'll know where we stand. It's a good thing we hadn't left when the call came through—I *might* just be able to persuade him to take that bloody plane away. . . ."

As he walked quickly towards the office, Johan cast his mind back to the only time he had heard Richter's voice, when he was in conversation with Bjerkelund the night before, and again when he had called across to his sergeant. A stern voice it was, but pleasant; the voice of a man in his late twenties, with a military ring about it. He gave the station-master a reassuring wink, and picked up the receiver.

"Richter," he said, non-committally.

"This is Major Holst," announced a stern voice at the other end in German.

"Good morning, sir," replied Johan, in the same language. "I'm still waiting for orders; we're completely isolated here."

"You're a fool, Richter," replied Holst gruffly. "Why haven't you contacted me again?"

"I tried, sir. But the telephone service in this godforsaken country is most inefficient."

"You can't have tried hard enough. We had to send a reconnaissance plane over to see what you were doing. High Command does not like being made to waste time and manpower in this way. I understand you've taken over the Swedish train. Is the cargo gold or ammunition?"

"Ammunition, sir. I reported to you last night that it might be gold because the Swedish driver said so, but it turned out that he was only joking."

"You examined the cargo very thoroughly, I trust?"

"Of course, sir. But we found it to be exactly as stated on the consignment papers. Ammunition."

"Hm. Well, you should have examined it as a matter of course."

"We *did* examine it! Our instructions were to search for the King of Norway; it was clearly impossible for any man, let alone that man, to be packed in a small box!"

"Don't be impertinent! . . . Have you found out from the driver where the secret destination was that he claimed the train was bound for?"

"No, sir. He wouldn't say."

"Hm. . . . Why did you take it upon yourself to detain the train?"

Johan hesitated, while he cast round wildly in his mind for a credible explanation. Luckily, the exact truth was lying at hand.

"The driver was drunk, sir," he replied, rather stiffly.

"Drunk?"

"Yes, sir. Acting in accordance with general orders to treat pro-German neutrals with politeness, my Sergeant invited him to come and have a drink in the station-master's office. He got very drunk in an unbelievably short time, and was quite unfit to drive. Actually, he's still asleep now."

"Then you will wake him at once! I have orders for you from Oslo. We have attempted to ascertain who gave him his original orders, but as no one important seems to know anything about it, we have decided to make use of the cargo ourselves. That train is to go immediately to Andalsnes, and you will accompany it. A large parachute drop has been organized to take over the whole harbour to prevent the British from landing there, and the ammunition will come in very useful for our troops."

"Yes, sir. What time is the drop?"

"At two o'clock precisely. You will be there ten minutes afterwards. Do you need help?"

"No, don't send any help," said Johan hastily. "There are too many foreign soldiers about; parachute troops would stand no chance of landing safely. Also, will you please tell the reconnaissance plane to leave me alone; it's attracting attention to me. I've got three Norwegian collaborators working with me here, and they report that they've been asked questions about it. Order it to leave me alone, or someone will notice it's escorting me, and attack the train."

"If you had reported all information to headquarters at the proper time, it would not have been sent. And don't presume to dictate to me! . . . Richter, you are being extremely impertinent today—are you drunk, too?"

"Of course not, sir!"

"Then you will behave yourself. Here are your orders. It is now nineteen minutes past eleven; you will arrive at Andalsnes in precisely two hours and fifty-one minutes' time. The reconnaissance plane will return to base now, and later it will report your arrival at Andalsnes, *and the exact time to the second*. Understood?"

He rang off, and Johan realized that he was sweating. He took off his cap and mopped his face with his handkerchief, and then he noticed that Carl was looking at him anxiously.

"We haven't a moment to lose," Johan said. "The Germans plan to attack Andalsnes at two o'clock; I'll have to get a warning down to the marines there. . . . Station-master, do you happen to know the telephone supervisor at Dombas personally?"

"Well, no, but I'd recognize his voice. There are only two operators at Dombas."

"Ask him to confirm that his exchange is in Norwegian

G

hands. One can't be sure of the position from one moment to the next, and I have an important warning to get through to Andalsnes; I'll code it. And you might ask him why he put through that German's call at all—there's no point in helping the enemy. Richter might easily still have been here."

The station-master called the exchange, and first of all satisfied himself that it was in the hands of the proper authorities. The operator sounded very upset; he had put the call through, he said, because there was a German sergeant breathing down the Dovre supervisor's neck, threatening to shoot him if he didn't co-operate. When he heard the actual conversation, he had been extremely worried, and had been planning to get a message down to Andalsnes himself. He would have phoned the harbour-master already, except that he had no authority; a message from him would carry no weight, and the officer who was given the message might just think it was some kind of German trick to distract the attention of the tiny Norwegian reserves from some other target.

"I have Captain Olsen here with me," the station-master told him. "He will draft a coded message to the military authorities at Andalsnes for you to send."

Johan took the receiver, and this time he spoke to the operator in Norwegian. "Richter was here yesterday," he confirmed, "but we—er—removed him. It was I who spoke to Major Holst just now. . . . The station-master says you overheard the conversation, and will send a message from me to Andalsnes. I want you to get through to Colonel Hagen, officer commanding marines at Andalsnes, at once."

"Yes, of course. What shall I say?"

"We'll warn him, of course, but I'll code the message. Stand by while I work it out." He rang off and coded his message in a few moments. However, like the telephone operator, he realized that his name would be unknown to Colonel Hagen; he had never worked closely with the marines. And so for the first time, and confident that it would convince Hagen of the authenticity of his message, he signed it with his code-name, 'Fridtjof'.

He then thanked the station-master for his help, and told him casually that there were a few dead Germans in one of his coal-bunkers. He glanced at his watch; it was just twelve o'clock. The Germans, he supposed, would not expect him to go faster than thirty miles an hour with an ammunition train; to reach Andalsnes at ten past two, therefore, they would expect him to leave Dombas in about ten minutes' time.

He hurried to the train and explained the position to the men. "Where's Bjerkelund?" he asked sharply.

"He's still asleep, sir," said someone. "We've been trying to wake him up, but——"

Bjerkelund was very sound asleep, and no amount of kicking would wake him. Someone turned him over, and an empty bottle of schnapps fell out of his hand.

"Hell!" growled Johan. "He must have got a private store in the cab . . . Larsen, do you think you can manage?"

"Oh, yes, sir," replied Olaf, eagerly. "I'm very glad I've had a chance to try her out, though. And I'll be careful with the brakes."

Johan looked undecided. It seemed a great risk to take, to place themselves and their cargo in the hands of this boy. However, the Sergeant put his mind at rest.

"Don't worry about the lad, sir," he said. "He's a good, careful driver. I was in the cab with him while he was driving last night. If I'd had any doubts about him, I would have told you immediately."

"But how would you know?"

"I'm a railway guard, sir. I've worked on the railways all my life—except when I was in the army. I *could* drive myself, at a pinch, although I'd rather not—under the circumstances. But I know enough about it to tell whether a man knows what he's doing or not."

"Well, I must admit that's a load off my mind. This sort of thing," and he looked at Bjerkelund's recumbent form in disgust, "simply never occurred to me."

"Then, why——?" began Olaf.

"No time for chatter! You were taken on as train-driver; now's your chance to prove your worth. Now listen, Borg, if you're a railwayman, you must know the railways pretty well. Is there somewhere at Lesjaverk where we could hide safely, or would you recommend somewhere else?"

"You've—er—got a map, haven't you, sir? It would help to revive my memory."

Johan produced it, and Borg put on his glasses and studied it carefully, frowning as he did so. Suddenly his expression cleared. "Would you mind going on to a branch line?" he asked.

"Not if that plane's gone. Where had you in mind?"

"Here," said the sergeant, pointing. "Trollheim. As you see, the tracks cut north into the Dovre Mountains—we'd have to get on to the Trollheim line at Hvitby. In daylight, we could be off the main line and driving into the mountains in a few minutes."

"And Hvitby, I see, is only about seven miles from here, and Trollheim another six miles or so further on. There'll be tunnels along that line, I should think."

"Oh, yes, sir, two or three."

"That would give us cover if any plane came over. . . . Why Trollheim?"

"There's a siding there that could have been made for us," the sergeant told him. "There's a piece of track there that leads into a granite quarry; it was specially laid down to make for easy loading. The track goes right into the mountainside— there's sheer rock on both sides. They'd never spot us there from the air, not with our white tarpaulins on top of the trucks. We'd simply blend into the snow; we could stay there for weeks."

"Sounds perfect. We'd better leave at once."

Olaf got into the cab to drive, accompanied by two riflemen and Peter Bergstrom to stoke, and the six German helmets and overcoats were distributed among the men most likely to be seen. The men manning the machine-guns each carried a blanket with them so that they would not freeze, and be ready for instant action if necessary.

Johan stood beside the train and surveyed it thoughtfully. He was uneasy about travelling by daylight, but, since he had no choice, he was determined to eliminate any unnecessary risk. Both watches were to be on duty throughout the brief journey; it sounded as though, with a little luck, they might get some rest at Trollheim. As his eye fell on Olaf Larsen, it occurred to him that something was wrong, and after a moment he realized what it was.

"Larsen," he called, "you're supposed to be a Swedish

civilian driver, not a German soldier. Go and get Bjerkelund's clothes and put them on. Wrap him in a blanket. . . . Help him, some of you men. We should get a move on now, or we'll be late for the Germans' time schedule. We'll get going as soon as Larsen's ready. Off you go now, and don't forget his cap—that's most important."

When Olaf reappeared he had put on his white fur coat over Bjerkelund's clothes, but the ancient cap, set at a jaunty angle, altered his appearance amazingly. Johan, now satisfied that everything had been done to ensure that the train would survive possible encounters with the enemy, climbed on board after a last word with the station-master, and told Olaf to drive to Hvitby. It was just 12.15.

Olaf got up steam. His attention was so taken up with working out the proper ratio between required average speed and lost momentum on braking due to weight that he did not see a barricade of logs right across the line as soon as he should have done. Fortunately it was at the end of a long straight stretch of track; Olaf pulled up with a screech of brakes, and Johan was beside him in the cab in a flash.

"What's the trouble?" he asked.

Olaf pointed.

"Stay exactly where you are," said Johan. "No point in getting any closer; we don't want to give them the chance to shoot at us from behind a barricade. I wonder why on earth they want to stop us here."

They had halted fifty yards short of the barrier; no one appeared. Whoever had put it there had probably hoped that the train would come right up to it; now they would have to walk through the snow, and make themselves very conspicuous.

"Stay in the cab, Olaf," said Johan. "We'll wait for them to make the first move. I don't want any shooting unless it's necessary. Ringe, go and make that clear to the machine-gunners. I'd say no one intended to derail the train; no driver could have failed to see that barricade from a perfectly safe distance. It's probably only put there for a spot-check; I'll have a little chat with whoever it is, and then we can get on again."

They were not kept waiting long. Soon, in formation, about

twelve Germans, all armed with submachine-guns, appeared from behind the barrier, and started marching towards them. They did not have to come far before it could be seen from their uniforms that they were mostly Gestapo, including an officer. Johan was puzzled; why the double-check? The train was well up to time. He decided it was probably just another example of German thoroughness. A short talk, the barricade would be removed, and they would be on their way again. He climbed out of the truck, to be ready for them when they arrived.

"Lieutenant Richter?" demanded the Gestapo officer.

"Yes. What do you want? I'll be late if you delay me." He was standing on top of one of the gold trucks, idly tapping his boot with his cane, and there was what he hoped was just the right trace of irritation in his voice.

The Gestapo officer glared at him. "We've both got jobs to do," he said frigidly. "If you co-operate, you need not be held up for more than half an hour. After that, you'll just have to drive faster. I have been sent to search this train."

"For Christ's sake, what for? It's already been searched for the King of Norway, and for gold bullion. What are you looking for? The crown jewels?"

"I am aware that these searches have been made. However, while the army may be satisfied that the gold is not on this train, the Gestapo is not."

"Look, I searched myself. How many more times do I have to report that this train is carrying ammunition?"

"I am prepared to believe that you have searched personally, and that you have found ammunition. But the ammunition could be in the top boxes only. Have you searched *every single* box on the train? . . . No, I can see that you have not! I have been sent to make a thorough examination of the cargo by Himmler himself. In the first place, the Norwegian gold reserves are not in the Bank of Norway in Oslo—the vaults are empty. The gold must be somewhere, and this train is the only lead we have. We have therefore made careful inquiries about it, both in Norway and in Sweden. It left Sweden carrying spare parts from a car factory; we checked. We are told that at Lillehammer the train was unloaded on April 12, and reloaded with ammunition on the instructions of the German occupying forces. You confirmed this last night when you telephoned Major Holst. Now you may not know this, but our troops had not reached Lillehammer on the 12th. They are, however, there now, and the original consignment of motor-car parts has been found where they were off-loaded. This train was therefore reloaded by the *Norwegian* authorities, not by the German. Now do you understand why it is necessary to search every single box? Where are your men?"

"In different trucks," replied Johan vaguely. "I told them not to show themselves, as I had no idea at first who had blocked the line."

"Quite right. Anyhow, it's not them I wish to speak to, but your Swedish driver, Jonas Bjerkelund, who must have watched the train being reloaded, and who actually told you last night, although you chose to ignore him, that there was gold bullion on board it."

He turned to two huge Gestapo men who were standing behind him, and pointed at Olaf Larsen, who was still in the cab. "Bring him over here to me," he snapped.

Olaf was dragged from the cab. He had no idea what Captain Olsen would like him to say, so he would just have to endure being roughed up. The Gestapo men sensed his fear and grinned. They shoved him in front of their officer, each one firmly holding an arm.

"Well," said the officer, still speaking in German. "Where did they put the bullion?"

Olaf, with an eye on Captain Olsen, forced himself to look sullen. The question was repeated, but still he remained silent. He was unprepared for the sledgehammer blow which landed on his ear and sent him sprawling across the track, hitting his head on one of the rails with a sickening jar. For a moment he thought he had broken his neck. He vaguely heard the Captain calling Bjerkelund, and then calling him a second time, more urgently. Had he forgotten that the man was sleeping off a whole bottle of schnapps? Johan for his part was wondering when on earth Olaf was going to remember that he was supposed to be Bjerkelund, or had he been knocked senseless? And now Bjerkelund himself, the last person the train's crew wanted to hear from, woke up on hearing his own name. Harald Bergstrom, next to him, reacted quickly; his boot shot out and caught him a sharp kick in the face, and he relapsed again into unconsciousness, blood streaming from a cut lip.

As Olaf continued to lie where he had fallen, one of the Gestapo men advanced towards him, stood him on his feet and shook him like a rat. With an effort he remained standing, swaying slightly. "Answer Lieutenant Richter when he speaks to you!" bawled his tormentor.

Olaf looked across at Captain Olsen, and saw him through a slight haze; he was certainly staring in his direction—with a start, he recollected that he was supposed to be Bjerkelund.

"It's no use treating Bjerkelund like that," Johan said. "He's simple-minded."

Olaf was glad of at least this much indication of what was expected of him. He fixed a rather uncertain gaze on Captain Olsen, allowing his mouth to fall open vacantly. He shuffled his feet, and blew his nose with his fingers.

The acting was superb; Johan checked a wild inclination to laugh. Drawing a deep breath, he said, "Bjerkelund, I want you to cast your mind back to the time your train was re-loaded at Lillehammer by the Norwegians. If they put crates of gold on the train, you are to tell us which truck or trucks they put them into. These gentlemen are very anxious to know, as you can see, so don't make a mistake, or I shan't be able to stop them knocking you about again. Consider each truck carefully, and then give us your answer. . . . *Starting with this one!*" he added loudly, and he tapped significantly on the living-truck with his cane. "Understood?"

As the living truck was the first truck behind the coal tender, Johan felt reasonably sure that his urgent gesture would be meaningless to the Germans. But, from Olaf's expression, he feared it had been meaningless to him as well; he just went on staring at him with his mouth open.

"The trucks aren't all the same, Bjerkelund," he added desperately. "Maybe you could remember the difference in the *contents* if you tried very hard."

Olaf appreciated the Captain's ruse, and, groggy though he was, he forced himself to peer fixedly at each truck before finally raising a hand and pointing at the living-truck.

"You'd better be right," growled Johan, still in German.

"Now go and fetch a hammer and chisel from the cab and bring them to me."

Olaf got himself somehow to the cab as quickly as he could, and cast round wildly for a hammer and chisel. Quite probably, he thought, there would be no such thing, but there was a bag of tools; he picked this up, and went back and handed it to Captain Olsen.

"Right. Now get back to your cab and stay there," ordered Johan, seizing the chance of getting him out of harm's way. Olaf had just enough strength left to climb up once more, and then he sank thankfully on to the floor of the cab; he felt the bump on his head, and found that his hair and the whole of one side of his face were soaked with blood.

Meanwhile, Johan threw the tool-bag into the truck, shouting in German, "You there, start opening up those crates and be quick about it—not the top ones, you stupid bastards, the ones underneath."

"Your men were having a little sleep, were they?" inquired the Gestapo officer, sarcastically.

"Certainly not!" replied Johan, and then improvised, "They're manning a machine-gun. We found some among the cargo while we were carrying out our search, and I had one mounted at each end of the train."

"A sensible precaution," said the other. "But it was a pity you failed to find the gold!"

"We still can't be sure there is any," Johan reminded him, raising his voice so as to be heard above the loud sounds of hammering now coming from the truck. "They're getting the first crate open now—I'll just go and take a look."

He jumped nimbly down inside the truck, and encountered a circle of anxious faces. "Ringe," he whispered urgently, "I want your lot down this end, in two pairs—the rest of you keep well out of it. I'm going to lure the Germans in, so be ready for them. You're to kill them quickly and in complete silence."

They nodded. None of them had actually killed anyone before, but they were highly trained and utterly confident.

"Where's Astrup?" whispered Johan.

"Manning a machine-gun; I'll make the fourth man," offered Carl eagerly.

After a momentary hesitation, Johan said, "Thank you, Ringe," and then started glancing round the truck. "I'll have to make sure they come in at the right place," he murmured to himself. Then his eye fell on an empty food crate, which he picked up. "I'll use this to corral them," he said, and then put his head over the top of the truck.

"First time lucky!" he called in an excited voice to the German officer. "We've found gold already. Like to come and have a look?"

"Of course! . . . Come with me, some of you men."

Johan threw down the empty wooden crate he was holding on to the ground. "Use that for a step," he said, "as there isn't a platform."

Then he slid out of the way, and allowed the German officer to jump right into the arms of Eriksen and Schwartz, lying in the dark waiting for him. Ringe and Krefting were ready for the next man, and Johan, Borg and the rest of the team watched with horrified fascination as four men in succession were neatly, efficiently and cold-bloodedly murdered.

The hammering continued, but the soldiers left standing in the snow began to get restive. No talking could be heard coming from the truck, and after a while one of them, more suspicious than the others, suddenly ran forward and jumped lightly on to the next truck, from which vantage point he was able to see what was happening. His eyes took a moment to adjust to the dim interior, and then he drew in a quick breath, seized his submachine-gun from his shoulder, and fired at the Norwegian uniforms he could see at the far end of the truck. The hail of bullets was cut short almost as soon as it began as Johan fired at him twice at point-blank range.

The rest of the soldiers, galvanized into action by the shooting, made a rush for the truck, and were caught in a withering cross-fire from the machine-guns at either end of the train. Only two were quick enough to escape, and these fled into the pine-forest which came right down to the railway track, and were instantly hidden among the trees. They had no intention of giving away their positions by shooting at an enemy they could not even see, so both sides held their fire. In the moment of silence which followed, Johan glanced round the truck. "Any casualties?" he whispered.

Everyone looked round in the gloom, and then there was a cry from Rolf Bergstrom, "Peter! Peter, are you all right? Peter, speak to me!"

Harald Bergstrom forced his way through the litter of dead Germans and frightened men to where the twins had been sitting, and picked up Peter's still form in his arms. He held him for a moment, his ear on the boy's heart. Then he turned and looked blankly and unbelievingly at Johan. "Sir," he said, "Peter's dead. Peter, my brother!"

There was a sharp burst of firing from the top of the slope, and a voice called in Norwegian, "Captain Olsen, are you all right? We got them both."

Johan peeped cautiously out of the truck. "Who are you?" he called back.

"Hvitby rifle club."

"Come on down."

They all watched as three men came skiing down to them through the fir-trees, rifles on their backs. "We watched the whole thing," said one. "We thought for a while that you were going to talk yourselves out of it, but then something went wrong. The two soldiers who hid behind the trees were easy targets for us. . . . How's that poor driver of yours?"

"Sergeant, send a couple of men to fetch Olaf," said Johan. "He's got a nasty cut on his head. . . . There are only three of you?" he asked the riflemen.

"Only three at this particular place. As soon as the message came from Dombas, we were all telephoned and told to get down to the railway as quickly as possible, so of course we're scattered all along the line. We heard the train coming as we got into position, and expected to see you pass. But you stopped suddenly. And then we saw the Germans."

At that moment, Olaf was brought out of the cab. He was only bruised apart from the cut on his head, and he grinned at Johan.

"Olaf, that was a marvellous performance!" he said. "How are you feeling?"

"Not too bad, sir!"

"Take him inside, you men, and give him a bit of first-aid treatment."

"It doesn't look as though he'll be able to drive, sir," said one of the Hvitby men. "Shall we telephone and ask for a driver to be sent out to you?"

Johan was beginning to worry about the time factor; if they were late, the spotter plane would come in search of them, and see them driving along the branch line. "My man can drive the two miles or so to Hvitby," he said. "Then we'll see."

He expected Bjerkelund to be able to help Olaf to drive the last six miles to Trollheim if necessary; if not, they could pick up a driver at Hvitby.

As they were talking, some of the crew were busy collecting the submachine-guns from the dead Germans lying on the track, and the Gestapo uniforms, and they rolled the corpses to the edge of the forest and covered them with snow.

As Johan climbed into the truck, he heard the Sergeant saying, "Bergstrom, you didn't need to have kicked Bjerkelund quite so hard."

"Didn't I?" snapped Harald. "Who got us into this bloody mess? Who told the Germans about the gold? If I had my way, I'd shoot him!"

Johan bent over Bjerkelund, and then noticed that blood was streaming from his chest as well as his mouth. Bjerkelund was dead. "You won't have to, Harald," he said shortly. "The Germans have done it for you. He must have caught the full force of that machine-gun burst. Only one other man was hit—your brother, Peter."

Rolf was crying in a corner of the truck; Johan patted him awkwardly. Schwartz and Krefting were just finishing bandaging Olaf's head.

"Are you fit to drive to Hvitby, Olaf?" asked Johan. "It's only two miles."

"I'll manage all right," said Olaf. "I hope! But isn't Bjerkelund awake yet?"

"Bjerkelund's dead."

"Well then, I'll have to manage," said Olaf, standing up rather unsteadily. "Will you come in the cab with me, Sergeant?"

"Of course, lad. And I'll watch how this new-fangled thing works, so that maybe I can take it to Trollheim myself. . . ."

Sir, those logs are still on the line. We should have told the rifle-club to move them."

"Well, we didn't! . . . Corporal Bergstrom, take three men and get those logs off the track. It's a quarter to one already, and we've only gone five miles!"

Harald, reminded of his responsibilities, pulled himself together with a visible effort. He chose three men, and the four of them started off at a fast lope towards the barricade. Rolf stood up and watched his remaining brother anxiously. Suddenly he tensed, and then let out three sharp whistles. Harald raised a hand in acknowledgement, and all four vanished immediately among the trees.

"You young idiot!" barked Johan, exasperated. "Sit down, if you can't bear to watch him, but for God's sake don't interfere. Can't you see the line must be cleared at once?"

But before he could shout to Harald to come out and get on with it, Rolf clapped a hand on his shoulder. "Quiet!" he hissed unceremoniously. "Look up there. Don't you see it?"

"See what?"

"Snow falling from a tree. The Germans must have put a scout up there—he's out of range of the train, but he's very close to the barricade, where they expected us to be! He could have shot them all easily."

As he was speaking, his arm was well over the side of the truck, and he was pointing steadily towards a certain place. "We can't see Harald," he said, "but he can see us. Now that he knows where to look, he'll get that man. Just you wait."

Johan was just as sure as Rolf that whoever was lurking up there was a foreigner; no Norwegian, collaborator or otherwise, creeping through a forest in winter would get close enough to a tree to shake snow off it—they had all learnt not to do that by the time they were five years old, playing 'cops and robbers'. Then there was a slight fall of snow from another tree, further down the slope, and instantly Harald and the three men with him all fired their rifles. A lot more snow fell then, as a grey shape rolled several feet downhill, till it finally came to rest. As it fell, the sound of a car's engine starting up came to everyone's ears, and they heard it being driven off quickly in low gear.

Harald came out of the forest at once with two of the men

and cleared away the logs, leaving the fourth in hiding, covering for them while they worked. He reappeared and joined them as they trotted quickly back through the trees to the train.

"Thanks, Rolf," panted Harald. "That bastard would have got the lot of us. . . . Sir, there was a man sitting in a car watching us while we were working. Directly that soldier fell, he took off. D'you think he was spying on us?"

"I don't see why he should have been; all the rifle club were told to keep an eye on us. He was probably one of them. . . . Olaf, off to the cab now as quick as you can; it's five minutes to one. You can have a long rest after this final effort."

"Come on, Peter," called Olaf. "Come and stoke my engine."

"Peter's dead," said Rolf, in a strangled voice.

"What!" wailed Olaf, leaning against the side of the truck. "Who else is dead? Tell me, I want to know!"

"Nobody else," replied Johan, sharply. "Larsen, pull yourself together for Christ's sake! We've got to get the hell out of here or we'll all be dead, and they'll get the gold after all our trouble. Astrup, go and stoke for him."

Borg stood beside Olaf while he drove, taking careful note of everything he did, learning how the modern engine worked, and ready to take over after the first few minutes should Olaf show any signs of faintness. One more corner, he told himself, and then they would have to start slowing down in order to stop opposite the platform.

He gave the order at exactly the right place, but there was no reaction. "Larsen, I told you to brake," he said, his voice sharp with anxiety. "Brake at once, or you'll never stop her in time."

"Can't you see I'm trying to!" cried Olaf desperately. "The brake's useless—it just won't answer!"

"Well, shut off steam then, for God's sake! . . . That's right."

They were passing through the station already, and Olaf caught a glimpse of astonished faces as he went straight on, and heard shouts of protest. Then he was aware that Captain Olsen was in the cab, and the Sergeant was explaining to him about the brake. "Be very careful on this corner, Larsen,"

Borg said to him. "After that she should come to a halt on her own; there's a slight gradient. . . . Ah, just as I thought."

The train came gradually to a standstill just out of sight of the station, drifted backwards a few yards, and then stopped again.

"Sorry, sir," whispered Olaf.

"Not your fault," said Johan. "But will one of you get us back to that station on the double!"

The Sergeant glanced at Olaf and saw that he was trembling. "I'll take her," he offered. "Larsen, how the devil d'you put this bloody thing into reverse?"

Olaf showed him, and they reversed with extreme caution back to Hvitby station, shutting off steam again some distance before they reached it, so as not to overshoot the mark a second time.

The whole of the station staff and some of the rifle club were waiting for them. "That boy's simply not fit to drive," protested the station-master, outraged at such an extraordinary performance. "I could easily have sent a man back from here."

"It's not the driver that's at fault, but the brakes," said the Sergeant. "Check all the air-brakes and be quick about it. We've got to make a dive for cover."

Faults were found in the brakes of two of the trucks, and while they were being adjusted Johan chafed at the delay. The damage had been done, he realized, when Olaf had pulled up so suddenly at the Gestapo block, and no one had had a moment to think of the probable result at the time. But it was now a quarter past one, and they were still only seven miles from Dombas, and a very long way from Andalsnes. He scanned the sky continuously but no plane appeared; with any luck it might be a little while yet before the enemy thought of searching as far east as Hvitby.

Another precious few minutes went by as they shunted the train on to the branch line, and then at last they were ready to start. Rudolf Borg told the captain he was perfectly capable of driving, and that he knew the line.

As they pulled out, Emil whispered to Harald, "Look, there's that car again. It's just driving into the station yard."

"So it is," said Harald. "Well, that proves he's a Hvitby man, like Captain Olsen said, so we needn't have worried."

NINE

DEATH OF A TRAITOR

"WE'RE JUST GETTING into Trollheim now." Johan glanced at his watch and saw it was five past two; the enemy would most certainly have started looking for them by now. . . . The Sergeant took the train down to his chosen hiding-place; as he had promised, the siding could have been made for them. He drove right down to the end of the line and halted at the granite face; on both sides were perpendicular cliffs, topped by snow and fir-trees; the camouflage was perfect. Hidden in the very heart of the mountain itself, there was no wind; it was in every way an extremely snug hideout. As soon as the train stopped, the machine-gunners hopped to the ground and climbed into the living-truck, and also Astrup and the two riflemen who had been on watch in the cab, and the Sergeant, looking very pleased with himself.

"Well done, Borg; this place is everything I had hoped for," Johan told him enthusiastically. "It begins to look as though we'd given them the slip. We'll all get some sleep as soon as we've had a meal; we only need two men on duty, and they're to watch for spotter planes, and report whenever they see one. Remember that they should have started looking for us already."

"Sir," said Carl tentatively, "all those dead bodies——"

"Yes, I see what you mean. Someone should go up to the station and arrange to have them taken away."

"The station-master's coming down now," said Borg. "I can see him. Actually, I recognize him; he's called Hvaldal."

Astrup and Krefting took off the extra overcoats and headgear from the German bodies, and Astrup said, "That Gestapo officer was a big man, sir. His coat will fit you much better than Richter's."

"I might need it yet."

When Hvaldal reached the train the Sergeant went out to

meet him. "Why, it's you, Mr Borg!" he said. "What a pleasant surprise. I was told by Hvitby to look after this train, and give you all possible assistance. Please tell His Majesty I have arranged accommodation for him and his staff here in the town. That's an excellent hideout for his train; I'd say it would be impossible to see it from the air."

"We're not carrying the King," said Borg. "Whatever gave you that idea?"

"Well, then, if it isn't the King, it must be the gold."

Rudolf Borg gave him a sharp look. "Come on board and meet Captain Olsen," he said.

Hvaldal got into the truck and looked about him. Men with rifles were sitting all over the floor, looking at him suspiciously, some in German uniform and some in Norwegian uniform, and his eye fell on a pile of dead bodies. He suddenly felt nervous. A huge, heavily built man dressed as a German lieutenant came forward, whom Borg introduced as Captain Olsen. "This is Bengt Hvaldal, sir," he said.

"Hvaldal," asked the giant tentatively, "what makes you think there's gold on this train?"

"All the stations know that the King is travelling on one train and the gold on another," was the reply. "So if you aren't guarding His Majesty, you're guarding the gold."

Johan just said, "Yes, the gold is on this train, and the enemy, I'm sorry to say, knows it, due to a series of unfortunate incidents. I asked Borg where was the best place to hole up for a while, and he brought us to Trollheim. Adolf Hitler permitting, we'd like to rest here for the next couple of days."

"Certainly, sir. Shall I send a few riflemen down to guard the train?"

"Better not. The enemy will already have planes in the air searching for us, and guards just might attract their attention. I'm hoping we've thrown them off the scent."

"Very well. Anything else I can do?"

"We need a baggage truck to take away these dead bodies, and some fresh food would be really welcome. I'll send a couple of men up with you."

"I'll go," said Harald Bergstrom. "Emil, you come with me. . . . And Knut, see that Rolf eats something."

H

Harald was beginning to find the sight of his brother's woebegone appearance an almost unbearable strain; there was no chance of his being able to comfort him when there was no privacy of any kind on the train; he therefore took the opportunity of getting away for a while with a friend of his own age in order to master his own grief at Peter's death, leaving Rolf in the sympathetic hands of Knut and Olaf.

The two elder brothers went up towards the station with Hvaldal. Suddenly one of the guards called, "Spotter plane overhead, sir. Very high."

Johan put his head out to look. "It's circling," he commented. "It couldn't possibly see us from there. Or could it?"

The plane continued circling, still very high, and one by one more men put their heads out to look. And then it flew off towards the east.

"Well, that's the first one, and it's missed us," said Carl. "I expect they're circling round all the stations."

Then the plane was back, this time circling much lower. Suddenly, it dived. It approached at full throttle, levelled off and flew, tree-top high, straight along their hidden siding. And then they saw it bank and, far too late, try to gain height to clear the steep quarry. A series of explosions, followed by flames and thick black smoke, marked the spot where it struck the ground.

Harald and Emil, with the station-master, were halfway up to the station when the plane roared down towards them. Instinctively they threw themselves to the ground, and then raised their heads to watch. As they lay, Harald's eyes were attracted by something bright red that he could see against the snowy background through the belt of fir-trees that separated the siding from the road. Somebody was standing in the middle of the road wearing a red cap; he was staring fixedly at the plane, and something which shone brightly was in his hand. The spectacle and the din of the crashing plane occupied their whole attention for a moment, and it was only in the silence which followed that they became aware of the sound of a car's engine; there was a car parked by the side of the road just opposite to them with its engine running, and it was the same car that they had already noticed twice before that day. The man in the road was now dashing to-

wards the car, his red cap in his hand; in a moment he would
be gone again. The one thought in Harald's mind was to catch
this man at all costs; it was clear to him now just how the
enemy had found the train so easily.

"Oh no, you don't!" he growled savagely. "Not this time—
we're due for a little chat!" and taking careful aim with his
rifle, he shot one of the back tyres of the car. The man paused,
cast a startled glance in the direction of the train, from
whence he clearly thought the shot had come, and fled from
it into the trees, straight towards the place where Harald and
Emil were lying on the other side of the narrow strip of
woodland. Once safely hidden, as he thought, he stopped
running, dropped to his knees and began crawling into thicker
cover; the two young men, invisible in their white coats,
crawled after him, signalling to Hvaldal to stay where he
was.

"Why don't you shoot him?" whispered Emil.

"Because I want a word with him! I'll go and get him now;
you cover for me."

As soon as he was close enough, Harald sprang on to the
man's back, but he quickly discovered that the stranger was
much tougher than he looked. Only Emil's timely intervention
prevented the spy from getting away a third time; Harald
was definitely getting the worst of the struggle when Emil
charged up swinging his rifle, and struck the man a hefty
blow on the head.

It wasn't necessary to bring their victim further than out of
the trees; everyone on the train had heard the shot after the
plane-crash, and Johan was on his way to investigate. Hvaldal
rushed to meet him, shocked and angry. "Your young thugs
have killed a man!" he cried. "They——"

"Oh, belt up!" Harald interrupted him rudely. "Sir, this is
the man we saw at the Gestapo block, and we saw him again
at Hvitby station——"

"You didn't report that to me."

"No, sir, because you said he was probably a member of
the Hvitby rifle club, so when we saw him at Hvitby——"

"All right, carry on."

"He was wearing this red cap, sir, and signalling to that
plane with something bright, and there's his car over there,

with the engine still running. I shot one of the tyres, so that he couldn't get away."

"So it wasn't the man you shot?"

"No, sir! He's still alive."

"He's not, you know," said Johan, who had been looking at their victim as he lay on the ground. "What was he signalling with?"

"I expect it's in his pocket." He put his hand into the man's right-hand jacket pocket, and brought out a magnifying hand mirror.

"Probably this, sir," he said, "don't you think?"

Johan faced the glass upwards, and it sparkled and shone in the bright sunlight. "Yes, this would be it," he said. "And a red cap," he added bitterly. "The one thing that could be relied on to be visible for miles on a white landscape! No wonder there was just the one spotter-plane——"

"I apologize for what I said about your men," said Hvaldal. "I thought——"

"Never mind," said Johan, "Just a misunderstanding."

"Well, hadn't I better send down some extra guards now, since the Germans know where you are? They'd be most unlikely to send down parachutists in broad daylight, after their previous experiences, but one can't count on it."

"Yes, we'll need extra guards at this stage," said Johan. "But perhaps you'd ask them to stay on the station. That way they can keep out of sight."

"Very well. And I suppose you'll be moving on after all, sir. No use staying any longer now they've found you, is it?"

"No. I'll move at dusk. I'll try to arrange to drive straight to the coast, but if I can't do that, I'll have to get the bullion off the train. If I should need lorries, can you get some at short notice?"

"Nothing easier. For a start, there are several belonging to this quarry, which are specially designed for carrying heavy loads. And you'd need a lot of men, too, wouldn't you?"

"I would. But presumably those could be got at short notice, too?"

"Certainly."

"Well, there's no need to mention it to anybody unless

they're actually needed. I'll be able to let you know definitely at about half past five."

"Very good, sir. Well, these two lads and I will get on up to the station, then, and bring down some fresh food and water on a trolley, and take away those corpses; there's an extra one of those now, too. . . ."

"Yes, do that. . . . Well, now we know exactly where we stand. Well done, you two."

Johan was left standing looking thoughtfully down at the dead man. "Why not go through his pockets, sir," he heard the Sergeant's voice. "It could be interesting to know who he was and where he came from."

They found a pocket-book and some letters; he was a Norwegian, Fredrik Kraft, but the most interesting discovery was that he lived in Dovre. "I'm afraid I can't have completely convinced Major Holst on the telephone after all!" said Johan, rather ruefully. "So he put a tail on us."

"Either that, or they thought it would be less wasteful, or less obvious, or both, than sending up aircraft. . . . Just a moment, here's a telephone number, written on the back of a cigarette packet. Dovre 295. That wouldn't be his own number, would it?"

"Hardly—on the back of a cigarette packet! And the packet's practically full; he must have only just jotted it down. I wonder whether Dovre's still in German hands; it would be worth checking that number."

They walked the rest of the way up to the station, and Johan picked up the telephone and asked for the Dombas exchange. "Dombas," he said, "this is Captain Olsen. I spoke to you this morning, do you remember?"

"Yes, of course. I got your warning through to Colonel Hagen personally at Andalsnes."

"Thank you very much indeed. Tell me, do you happen to know if the Dovre exchange is still held by the Germans?"

"I'm afraid it is. The situation is very fluid at the moment——"

"Never mind. Listen, I'd like to check a number in Dovre; I think it's quite likely that a German will answer, and I want to make sure. Please explain to the Trollheim exchange that I am an army officer, and am merely ringing this number as a routine inquiry. And tell them not to worry about the conversation. If it's an enemy-held number, as I hope, then my intention is to give them some false information."

"I heard that," said another voice. "This is the Trollheim exchange. Thank you, Dombas! . . . I'll put your call through to Dovre, Captain Olsen. What number do you want?"

"Dovre 295, please."

"295? Well, that's an odd coincidence! I put a call through to that number less than an hour ago; it's definitely an enemy-held number."

"The caller's name wouldn't be Fredrik Kraft, would it?"

"Yes, that was his name! He started speaking in Norwegian, but was asked to speak German—his Dovre contact found him difficult to understand. I would have cut him off normally, but yesterday Dovre was added to the list of towns to which all calls must be put through and monitored, as people are still phoning in false reports as to the King's whereabouts. Half the town's been taken over now, and they still have the exchange. As it happens, this call could easily have been about the King—he mentioned a vehicle."

"What exactly did he say?"

"He said the vehicle in question was at Trollheim, just that."

"And the answer?"

"Nothing much. They just thanked him, and rang off."

"Well, your information couldn't be more welcome," Johan told him, "because Kraft is the person I have to pretend to be. So perhaps you could tell me what his voice sounded like."

The operator laughed. "Kraft has a broad Opland accent—like mine," he said. "You would have given yourself away the moment you opened your mouth! The accent came through clearly even in German, so remember that all the time you're speaking. Shall I put you through now?"

"No. I'll call you back in a few minutes. I'll have to make up my mind what to say."

Johan put down the receiver and explained things to the sergeant. "Kraft can't have reported the plane crash at Dovre," he said, "because he had no chance of getting to a phone before he was killed. The pilot presumably came down to have a look for himself, because he couldn't possibly have seen us from where he was. Stupid thing to do really, since the whole idea of employing Kraft would have been to lull us into a false sense of security."

"He was probably told to check for certain," said Borg with a grin, "and, with teutonic thoroughness, he did so!"

"Probably. Well, we must see that Dovre doesn't guess we've been alerted. Then we can prepare a reception committee for them. The whole of Trollheim can be on the station to meet them!"

"Do you intend to stay here tonight, sir?"

"Christ, no! Not after what's happened. I hope to be able to run straight down to Andalsnes by train after dark. I'll phone Hagen at about half past five—I don't want to ring sooner than that, because he's got a battle on his hands today, as you know. Now that the allies have started to land, it's quite possible he may have arranged transport for the gold to England already. I think I'm ready to ring Dovre now."

He got through to Dovre 295, and merely said, in Norwegian, "This is Fredrik Kraft speaking."

'One moment," replied a voice. "I will fetch Major Holst at once."

Johan's nerves began to tingle as he realized he was about to speak to Holst for the second time that day. When he finally heard the one word, "Holst," announced in the same gruff, business-like tone as before, he stumbled quickly into his prepared speech, but in an Opland accent so thick that Major Holst had to ask him to repeat himself. Noting that there was no sign of suspicion in the voice, he was able to speak much more confidently the second time.

"Sir, have you been informed of my precise location?" he asked. "I thought you'd be sending for further information. Your messenger hasn't called again."

"I received all details in his first report," said Holst. "And you may speak freely—Dovre is now in the hands of the German army. Everything is poised for the battle for Dombas tomorrow."

He sounded very excited; there was clearly no room in his mind for doubts as to the authenticity of his caller. "Are you trying to tell me that my plane hasn't been back for a second look? And for God's sake speak German."

"Yes, sir," said Johan, switching to German, "that's why I telephoned."

"Well, it doesn't matter, since your information, which he relayed to me, was quite clear the first time. I have found the siding on my map. But he should have returned some time ago—he probably got over-confident and crashed in the mountains. Bloody fool. Did you manage to get up to the station and find out what they are intending to do tonight?"

Johan had prepared a little speech on this subject, but this was a perfect cue; all he had to do was answer the question, and Holst would have no reason to disbelieve him. "They are going to spend all night and tomorrow at Trollheim," he said. "They are all extremely tired, and the Gestapo killed several of their men during the fighting near Hvitby, so there are only a few of them left to guard the train. They didn't say where they planned to go next, but they sounded very confident that they had shaken you off."

"So they didn't notice the reconnaissance plane?"

"They noticed it, yes, sir. But they decided it was too high up to see them. Which of course it was."

"Very well, Kraft. Thank you. And you're quite sure there's gold on that train?"

"There must be, sir. I heard the Gestapo officer say so—he checked. But then he was killed, and——"

"Keep them under observation until I get there, and then when the bullion is in our possession, you can come back to Dovre with it."

He rang off; Johan took two deep breaths, and then turned to Borg.

"He didn't suspect you?" asked the Sergeant.

"No."

"What'll you do if you can't get to Andalsnes, sir?" asked Borg.

"Shift the bullion on to lorries. We'll drive off and be well away before dawn. Hvaldal will arrange for Holst's parachutists to be greeted in a suitable manner!"

"I don't think there'll be any parachutists tonight," said the Sergeant, looking towards the south-west. "The sky's pretty heavy to windward; it'll probably be snowing in half an hour."

When Johan went up to the station to telephone Colonel Hagen it was already snowing quite heavily. The sky was black and lowering over the Jotenheim Mountains to the south-west, promising snow for at least several hours. It took the operator some time to get through to Andalsnes dockyard, but eventually a deep voice said, "Hagen speaking."

"Colonel Hagen, this is 'Fridtjof'."

"Ah, 'Fridtjof'! Thanks very much indeed for your warning; your message came just in time to allow us to get reinforcements—they dropped three to four hundred men at about two o'clock, as you said . . . I hope you haven't phoned to say you're in trouble yourself?"

"I'm in rather a tight corner," said Johan cautiously. "I was hoping to be able to come down to you tonight."

"You can't possibly do that. The whole place is swarming with parachute troops! Can't you wait for forty-eight hours? In this weather, a couple of nights in the open should finish them off."

"I'll have to move from here tonight, anyhow."

"Hm. Where are you?"

"At Trollheim. And if I can't get down to you at once, I'll have to go back on the road."

"The *road*! Well, you know best." Hagen thought for a moment. "You might join the Fifth Division for a bit," he suggested, "if you could make your way back to Dombas and pick up a British escort going north. Or if you can't do that, go to a logging camp somewhere in the mountains and send a messenger to Fifth Division telling them where you are. But whatever you do don't come down here. Fourth Division's mounting a major operation at once to clear out pockets of the enemy in the town of Andalsnes and in the dockyard itself. Some of the Germans are wearing Norwegian uniforms collected during today's fighting and we must get ourselves sorted out while there's still enough daylight left to allow us to recognize our own men. But we're too short-handed to go chasing Germans hiding in the forest. These could be a real danger to you. Contact Fifth Division somehow, and then I'll drive up myself and have a talk with you, or send someone. I've—er—arranged transport for you. And thanks again for your timely warning today. We managed to hold the port, but if we hadn't had a chance to alert Fourth Division we would certainly have lost it. I'm only sorry I can't help you at once."

Johan went out into the driving snow and bellowed for Hvaldal; lorries and men, he said, were to be brought to the station on the double.

"You can't get to the coast, then?"

"Not yet, I'm afraid. So we'll have to get the stuff off this train."

TEN

THE GERMANS CAPTURE AN EMPTY TRAIN

JOHAN RETURNED to the train, and told the crew the news that they could not go to Andalsnes for another two days, to allow the marines, Fourth Division and the weather between them to reduce the number of parachute troops still at large near the port to an acceptable level. They were therefore going to unload the cargo on to lorries immediately, and hide with it in some remote logging camp for the night; tomorrow they would join the Fifth Division and await orders for shipment.

Next he asked Olaf if he was fit enough to shunt the train up to the goods shed and then take it back to the siding later, so that it would be where the Germans would expect to find it when they came looking for it—this would be his last chance to drive it. Olaf got into the train and reversed back to the station, no easy task in heavy snow.

They found the goods shed swarming with men; it was obvious that Hvaldal must have warned them well in advance, in spite of Johan's request for secrecy. He was there himself, looking like a conjuror who had just produced several rabbits out of a hat.

Johan asked him about lorries. "All in the quarry's own garages, sir, just down the road; they're beginning to bring them up now."

The loading and reloading of the gold proceeded smoothly and efficiently. Hvaldal had arranged for groups of men to rest in turn, and after working for an hour or so Johan went to take a rest himself. He noticed immediately that the snow seemed to be slackening. If the weather should clear for any appreciable period, he knew he could trust Major Holst to send over a reconnaissance plane, which would be able to report his every move to Dovre. He was relieved to see that snow was still banked up in thick clouds over the mountains—

the lull was only temporary. Nevertheless he went over to Hvaldal and asked him if there was any way of speeding things up a bit.

Hvaldal was sympathetic. "The men are no longer young," he reminded Johan. "If I tell them to hurry it, the rhythm will go wrong; there's no chance of any extra speed here. I know you're worried about planes, but as I see it you will be at your most vulnerable while you're actually on the road— you can't possibly drive in this sort of weather without head-lights. So why don't you plan on a very short journey? There's a large, unoccupied logging camp no more than three miles from here, deep in the forest. I'd make for that if I were you."

"Could we get the lorries under cover?"

"You could, certainly. There's garaging for all their own lorries there."

"In that case it sounds perfect." Hvaldal, Johan thought, was certainly a very useful man; if the weather proved as helpful as the Trollheim station-master tonight, he reckoned that by the morning the trickiest part of their journey would be behind them.

An important point suddenly occurred to Johan; he went across to see Olaf, who was keeping his engine hot for the return journey to the siding. "Olaf," he said, "do you think you would be able to disconnect the telephone exchange?"

"D'you mean go and tell the operator to switch it off, sir?"

"No, that wouldn't be good enough; I shouldn't be able to rest wondering if they'd reconnected it for what they might consider an important emergency. Nothing is more important at Trollheim at this moment than the gold reserves—but it's just possible that they might not see it that way. No, I was wondering whether you could think up some subtle way of disconnecting it yourself from the outside—some little fault that would be difficult to trace."

Olaf put down his coal shovel. "I might manage something from the inside, if I went in for a chat. I could take Eriksen with me; he's a good conversationalist. While he's chatting up the night operator, I could have a go."

The night operator was very pleased to see the two young men, and to hear at first hand what was going on; Olaf said that they had been sent by Captain Olsen. While Eriksen chatted, Olaf wandered unobtrusively round. After about five minutes, he made a great show of looking at his watch, and then said to Eriksen, "Come on, we can't chat here all night! We're expected back at the station."

He said good night hurriedly to the operator, dragging Eriksen after him.

"You disconnected something?" asked Eriksen.

"Something small that never usually goes wrong. Let's test it."

They went into a call-box, and Olaf picked up the receiver. "Dead as a door-nail!" he reported.

By the time they got back to the station they found that the job was finished, and the Sergeant had driven the train back in Olaf's absence; all their stores had been transferred to the lorries as well, and Hvaldal was waiting to see them off.

"Managed all right, did you?" Johan asked.

"Piece of cake," said Olaf proudly.

A local driver led the convoy of twelve lorries, and very soon they turned off the main road on to the logging track; if the snow continued to fall at its present rate, all tyre-tracks should be covered almost as soon as they were made.

At last the leading lorry turned off the main track, and came to a halt soon afterwards in front of the logging camp recommended by Hvaldal. If it had not been for their local guides, the team might well have driven straight past it in the blizzard. Johan ordered all the lorries to be garaged immediately.

The thirty or so Trollheim men volunteered to keep watch over the gold during the night.

Back in Dovre Major Holst had been far more relieved than Johan could know when he had received the fake call purporting to be from his spy, Fredrik Kraft. Johan had certainly noticed that he appeared to be in high spirits, but he had put this down to the fact that the Germans expected to take Dombas in the morning, after which he realized that they would be able to come west fairly rapidly, swallowing up the whole of south Norway—unless the allies landed sufficient troops and aircraft during the next twenty-four hours to oppose them. What he did not know was that Holst had suffered severe reprimands from practically every quarter for landing in Dovre with his paratroopers instead of Dombas; his excuse that the strong south-west wind had blown them away from the scheduled dropping-zone was not accepted anywhere, since a Major in the German army was expected to be sufficiently alert not to be affected by such things as weather conditions, however sudden and perverse. He was being held responsible for the fact that, due to his negligence, both the King and the gold reserves might very well have been able to escape through the bottleneck. The last thing, therefore, to occur to Holst when he received the satisfactory news that the gold was definitely on board the train which was standing at Trollheim station was that the call was not genuine.

It had been his own idea to employ Fredrik Kraft to follow Lieutenant Richter's train from Dombas; Richter's attitude, when he had spoken to him on the telephone while the train was at Dombas, had been disquieting—he had never before had to reprove an officer under his command for impertinence. He could not shake off the suspicion that Richter had been drinking, and he had clung to the possibility that there might be at least some gold on that train after all. Kraft, despatched half an hour after Holst's conversation on the telephone with Johan Olsen, impersonating Richter, had arrived in time to witness the train's arrest by the Gestapo, and the subsequent fighting, and he had managed to get back a message to Holst speaking in Norwegian from a call-box from Hvitby. Although Holst spoke quite good Norwegian, he found it difficult to understand Kraft's accent, so normally they spoke in German. For such a call, however, Norwegian had been essential; Kraft had spoken as clearly as possible, and the message, although obscurely worded, had been understood by Holst. Now, he had had two more messages from Kraft from Trollheim, and he was exultant. He would arrange a parachute drop over Trollheim tonight, and he would go with the men himself to ensure that nothing could possibly go wrong this time; he would capture the train, and force that Swede to drive it straight to Oslo.

Holst spent a happy afternoon looking forward to the

evening's surprise attack on the gold train, but at five o'clock
he experienced a sharp disappointment; his Sergeant called to
see him with the weather report. Heavy snow was rapidly
approaching the Heights of Dovre from the Jotenheim Mountains, and by half past five it was anticipated that all planes
would be grounded.

Holst was furious; somehow he must get to Trollheim that
night. How long was the snow going to last?

"Several hours at least, sir, I'm afraid," the Sergeant told
him. "But if you're determined to get there tonight, why not
go by car?"

"You're crazy! We'd run slap into the British army at
Dombas!"

"Not if you bypass Dombas. You can't bypass it to the
north, because the Norwegian Fifth Division and allied troops
are throughout that area, but you could bypass it to the
south, and then get back on to the main road just beyond
Rauma. Once on the main road, it's only about 14 miles to
Trollheim . . . I've brought a map, sir; perhaps you'd like to
have a look."

Holst beamed; Sergeant Schultz was a tower of strength.
Schultz had been at great pains to build up this image of
himself; Holst was a difficult man to work under, but he was
a good Nazi, and had sufficient pull in Berlin to be able to
make life rosy for those who pleased him. Together they
studied the map; the detour, although short, was mountainous
—a difficult road for private cars. And they would have to
use private cars, if they wished to avoid being lynched by
the inhabitants. But if they took plenty of men, the cars
could be pushed through snowdrifts if necessary. Schultz
departed to find four powerful cars, and twenty-two reliable
men, making a total of twenty-four. Holst, he knew, would
want to come himself, and he went nowhere without Her-
mann Schultz.

They would leave, Holst said, at seven o'clock. At half past
six, the full force of the blizzard reached Dovre. Holst, fuming,
decided to wait until the storm had slackened before setting
out. He had to wait until half past ten.

It took them three hours to get past Dombas on the treacherous mountain track. The narrow road was like a switchback,

and all four cars had to be pushed over the crest of each hill, after the deep snow had been shovelled away.

Holst reached Trollheim at about half past two in the morning. He and his men parked their cars about a quarter of a mile from the station; they intended to capture it first, so that there would be no chance of anyone skiing through the trees and warning the train's crew of their approach before they reached it. They did not know how many men were guarding the train—they could well find themselves outnumbered, so complete surprise was essential.

Holst spread his men in a circle round the station building, and they closed in on it gradually. Those who reached the station-master's office, the waiting-room and goods shed first threw open the doors and fired their submachine-guns into the dark interiors, ducking for cover immediately in the snow outside, and waiting for the sound of a cry, or a stumbling step. Nothing. They spent another ten minutes making absolutely sure that the buildings were all completely deserted, and then Holst called the men together, checked that everyone was present, and led them warily down through the narrow belt of woodland towards the siding where he had been told the train was hidden.

When finally its dark shape could be made out against the snow Holst told his men to pass down the order that as soon as they saw him jump into one of the trucks, they were all to leap into it after him. This plan, at any rate, would enable them to fight in a body, and from under cover. Choosing the truck directly above him, he leapt suddenly out from under the train into it, quickly joined by his men, who jumped in from both sides. The truck was completely empty; they squatted on the floor for a few moments listening, but they were still unchallenged.

At this point, Holst began to have definite misgivings. "Search the train," he snapped, "but don't separate. All of you search from here to the engine, and then, if you find nothing, try the other end of the train."

In a few minutes he knew the worst: the train was completely empty. Well, they couldn't have taken the gold away without lorries, and even if they had merely put it in the vault of the local branch of the Bank of Norway, everyone

Lillehammer

Railway line,
Gudbrandsdalen

The Rendal

Hjerkinn Station

Railway line near
Dovre

Dombas Station

in the town must know about it; he would soon find out where it was.

The Germans drove up into the town, and stopped. Holst told his men to force their way into the nearest houses and bring out the inhabitants; standing practically naked in the snow in the middle of the night, he reckoned they would probably tell him fairly quickly what he wanted to know.

When about fifty people, of all ages, had been assembled, Holst spoke to them in their own language, and ordered them to stand in lines; the soldiers stood in a row in front of their hostages, the machine-guns at the ready.

"Today a train came to Trollheim," stated Holst in his harsh accent. "It was carrying the Norwegian gold reserves. The gold is required by the German authorities to pay for the arming and fortifying of your country against attack by the British. We have just paid a visit to the station, and have discovered that the bullion has gone. It would have needed a great many men to shift so much gold. Tell me at once where it is, and then you may all return to your homes."

The Norwegians remained silent. The Major's harsh voice became harsher.

"We came to Norway to protect you against our mutual enemies," he said, "but you Norwegians are not grateful. Since you people of Trollheim appear to be just as unco-operative as the rest of your countrymen, we will show you that we have another side to our characters." He raised his voice to a bellow. "If I have not been given the information I seek by the time I have counted fifty, three of you will be shot!"

The Norwegians knew that this was no idle threat; people all over the country had already been shot for failing to supply information, often when they were quite unable to give it.

The Major was counting slowly; they all began to try to work out how much information would be acceptable to get themselves off the hook, without necessarily leading to the capture of the gold.

Bengt Hvaldal, standing in the front line with his wife and his two daughters, was the first to come up with a worthwhile inspiration. The idea which sprang into his mind was born of his previous misunderstanding that the train which the station-

I

master at Hvitby had asked him to look after was carrying
the royal party. If the Germans could be persuaded to look
for private cars, he thought, they would be unlikely to search
logging camps for lorries, and when they had gone he could
telephone Captain Olsen at his camp and warn him. The idea
of telephoning only occurred to Hvaldal when Holst had
reached forty-one in his countdown—that particular camp
had only recently had its telephone installed, which was why
he didn't speak up the moment the plan struck him, but this
fact clinched it for him.

"The gold hasn't been brought to Trollheim," he announced
rather shakily. "The train at the station was carrying the
royal party."

Holst stopped counting and glared at him. "The royal party?"
he repeated. "In a goods train? What kind of fool do you take
me for? You will be taught immediately that the German
army cannot be taken in by fairy stories. . . . Schultz!"

But Schultz was already at his elbow. "There could just be
something in what this man says," he said softly. "It was to
capture the King that you sent Lieutenant Richter to Dombas
in the first place—and *that* information was not fed to us
deliberately; we learnt that His Majesty was going in a train
to Dombas by listening in to a telephone call from the driver
of that very train!"

"But Richter himself mentioned gold——"

"He said the engine-driver was joking, didn't he? I suggest
that the King was aboard the train all the time, hiding among
the boxes. Goddammit, it's been done before!"

"Kraft's information would indicate that the cargo on the
train was, in fact, gold."

"But, sir, why should you trust an informer? Much safer
to believe a call we weren't meant to hear."

"And the Gestapo block?"

"Moonshine, probably."

"Then, Schultz," whispered Holst, "where is Richter? Just
tell me that!"

"It looks as though he had been murdered, sir, and all his
men; possibly at Dombas. You said his voice on the telephone
the next morning didn't sound normal. Don't you remember
that?"

"By Christ, I do! I thought he was drunk, but if it was someone else speaking——"

"Exactly, sir!"

"Well, then," said Holst briskly, "if we can't trust anyone, why should we believe this man's story that the King was on that train?"

"Ask him, sir. Just you ask him, and I'll make sure he tells you the truth!"

Hvaldal was hustled in front of Holst, losing a shoe on the way.

"Why are you volunteering this information?" asked Holst crisply. "Speak up and be quick about it."

"My wife and two daughters are in the front row, sir. To save their lives——"

"Quite, quite. You will now tell me why you, but apparently no one else here, knew what that train was carrying."

"Sir, I am the station-master."

"So?" Holst's eyes gleamed. "You are the station-master, are you? So you would know exactly what went on at your station?"

"Certainly." Hvaldal's self-confidence began to return.

"Then," roared Holst, seizing him by the collar of his dressing-gown, "you will tell me what the devil the King was doing in a goods train!"

"They said it was the only one they could get hold of," answered Hvaldal in a muffled voice.

"Hm." Holst let him go. "You will prove your story immediately," he snapped. "Lead us to the house where the King is sleeping."

This was a complication Hvaldal had not thought of, but it would make no difference if he stuck to the story he had invented.

"They didn't stay here," he said. "They borrowed three cars and drove away."

"How long ago?"

"Less than an hour. They waited for the moon to come out, so that they wouldn't have to use headlights."

"Which way did they go?"

Hvaldal pointed towards the forest track; there would, he knew, be vehicle tracks of some sort on it, and the Germans would be sure to find them, but it had been snowing heavily while the lorries were on the road, and he knew that most of the tracks would have been obliterated. The passage of three cars, he felt, could be held to account for whatever tracks were still visible.

Holst sent two soldiers to go and confirm that there were tracks on the road indicated. Vehicle tracks were clearly visible; by daylight, they would probably have been able to identify them as lorry tracks, but by the uncertain light of their torches the blurred outlines could just as well have been made by three heavy cars. They ran back and told the Major.

"Schultz," called Holst, "take some men round with torches and examine the other roads out of this rat-hole."

On completing his check, Schultz was able to report that there were no tracks to be seen on any other road leading out of Trollheim, except those made by their own cars. Holst was satisfied that whoever had left Trollheim that night could only have gone by the road indicated by Hvaldal.

"Where does that road lead to?" he asked.

"Nowhere special. It was built for tourists to see the mountains."

"Then where were they heading for?"

"His Majesty did not confide in me," replied Hvaldal with dignity.

Holst accepted this. "It doesn't matter," he said. "Such tracks should be easy to follow, and they won't have got far in thick snow. . . . What's your name?"

"Bengt Hvaldal."

"I am Major Heinrich Holst. I will see that you are rewarded for your co-operation."

When the Germans had driven off, everyone crowded round Hvaldal all talking at once, some congratulating him, and others loudly demanding to know what steps he proposed to take to protect the country's gold reserves.

"I shall warn Captain Olsen by telephone immediately," he said.

"That camp hasn't got a phone," said someone.

"Yes it has. It was put in a few weeks ago. I'll handle this; Captain Olsen knows my voice, and so does Mr Borg, so you can all go back to bed."

As soon as he arrived home with his family, he went straight to the telephone, but to his annoyance he found the line was dead. He went out into the snow again, and knocked on the door of the next house. His neighbour, who had only just got back, asked anxiously who was there.

"It's me, Bengt Hvaldal," came the answer. "My phone's out of order."

Hvaldal discovered immediately that this line was also dead —he assumed that the Germans must have cut the lines before leaving the town. There was nothing for it but to go to the exchange itself. The night operator tested the lines at once, and quickly realized that the whole exchange was out of order. Hvaldal's heart began to beat even more wildly; he was close to panic.

"Why the hell didn't you notice?" he shouted. "I have to put through a most urgent call!"

"Can't it wait till morning?"

"It can't wait five minutes!" And, stammering with desperation and distress, he managed, in a somewhat disjointed manner, to tell the whole story.

The night operator was alarmed.

"I'll go and fetch someone to mend it," he said.

The mechanic when he came was puzzled; he could find absolutely nothing wrong. Olaf Larsen had done his work well.

Hvaldal, looking at the time, realized it was too risky to wait any longer. If the logging camp could not be contacted by telephone, someone would have to go over there on skis. He ran back to his house, dressed himself in warm clothes, strapped on his skis, and started off through the pine forest.

ELEVEN

MOONLIGHT BATTLE IN THE SNOW

HOLST AND HIS MEN found the going along the forest track unexpectedly rough, but they persevered, reckoning that if the King's cars could be driven along that road, there was no reason why theirs shouldn't. They were in point of fact trying to drive over snow which had been crushed into thick ice by the passage of the gold lorries, but they did not realize this because of the light coating of snow that had fallen since, camouflaging the ice. They had covered nearly three miles when Sergeant Schultz glimpsed through the trees the outline of a log-cabin; there might not be another for miles. Holst must be worn out; he would offer token resistance to the idea of taking shelter, but only for form's sake; Schultz knew him well, and set his mind to thinking up arguments that Holst could accept out of apparent consideration for his men.

His first reply was exactly what Schultz had expected: "If the King can drive along this road, so can we!"

"But, sir," said Schultz, persuasively, "I was looking at it the other way round; in short, if we *can't* drive along this road, then *neither* can he! So he can't be far ahead, and his tracks are quite clear; with any luck, he has been unable to find shelter. So if we get the men warmed and fed in this hut, we can send them out in scouting parties in half an hour's time, and they'll probably find him fairly quickly."

Holst allowed himself to be persuaded, and the men ran towards the hut. They found a neat stack of logs next to the fireplace, and some of them immediately got a fire going while others closed the shutters and lit the paraffin lamp. Then they set up a cooking-stove, and were soon busy heating tins of food.

Meanwhile Carl Ringe, on duty at the logging camp, kept his ears strained for noise from the Trollheim men, as Rudolf

Borg had told him that if the noise they were making got worse, it would have to be stopped. Borg himself could not rest; at half past one the snow stopped completely, and he went outside to examine the tyre tracks by moonlight. For some time the noise was only slight—a low buzz of conversation and an occasional burst of laughter—but quite suddenly it redoubled, and then grew louder as more men joined in the shouting. This state of affairs was obviously what the Sergeant had feared, and Carl went straight over and woke Captain Olsen. Johan was furious; he leapt up, and, taking Corporal Schwartz with him, went over at once.

This disturbance had been caused by the arrival of Hvaldal, with his urgent news that German troops had arrived at Trollheim and were now in the forest looking for the train's cargo. He had heard the men talking from some way off, which was why he had gone to their cabin to report. As he poured out his story for the second time to Johan when he appeared with Schwartz, the men quietened down. Borg, standing in the snow with his hands in his pockets, decided to wait just a little longer until he was quite sure there would be no more outbursts. His Captain was only a young man; he had feared he mightn't be able to handle these old stagers.

As the Sergeant didn't return, Carl peeped through a chink in one of the shutters and saw him. "I wonder what Uncle Rudolf thinks he's doing," he said anxiously. "It's silly standing out there in the moonlight. Someone might see him."

"Well, call him in then," suggested Krefting. "You're an officer, aren't you?"

"You know I can't do that," growled Carl. "He'd sulk for days! . . . But you and Astrup could cut out by the back door and creep round and keep an eye on him—that's the best thing. There's plenty of cover."

Astrup and Krefting departed at once; this was the kind of assignment they enjoyed. They found a good place to hide, and lay down, watching their sergeant.

Carl Ringe was not the only one to observe Rudolf Borg's solitary vigil. Sergeant Schultz, only half a mile away, had not stayed in the Germans' hut long enough for a meal; as soon as his hands and feet were comfortably warm, and he had had a couple of pulls at his brandy flask, he told Major Holst that he was going out to follow the tracks of the royal cars at once; he felt certain that the other party could not be far away. As he opened the door, the sound of men's voices echoed clearly across to him through the silent forest. He called the major at once.

Together they stood in the doorway facing the sound; then Holst brought his field-glasses to bear in that direction. The first thing he saw clearly was the tall, slim figure of an elderly man with a military moustache wearing an army greatcoat, standing alone in the snow. His heart gave a wild leap.

"Schultz," he exclaimed, "that station-master was telling the truth after all. I can *see* the Norwegian King!"

"Let me have a look."

Schultz seized the binoculars, took one look and turned to Holst in delighted incredulity. "Sir, he's alone, and his men are drunk!" he whispered. "Can't we go and nab him at once, while the going's good?"

"It's worth a try," said Holst, his eyes glued to the binoculars. "Send four men on skis, but they'll have to walk back. If he gives trouble they'll have to knock him on the head and carry him—there's plenty of cover. But make sure they understand they're not to hit him too hard; I want him alive."

Astrup and Krefting, beginning to feel the cold in their hiding-place, were overcome with astonishment when four German soldiers on skis suddenly stepped out of the woods a few yards away from them, grabbed Sergeant Borg and hustled him into the undergrowth. Krefting was the first to recover. "Stay here," he whispered sharply, "and watch. I'll cut back and tell Carl."

The Germans were not speaking threateningly to Borg—on the contrary, they sounded inexplicably polite, and then, just as Krefting was leaving, they both distinctly heard one of them say, "Your Majesty."

"How absolutely fantastic!" whispered Krefting. "They think he's the King! Anyhow it looks as though they want him alive, so they won't harm him."

Rudolf Borg's first involuntary yell was stifled by a large hand over his mouth. Firmly held by three soldiers, so that he was practically unable to move a muscle, the fourth one addressed him. At first he couldn't believe his ears, but when he was obliged to believe that they really thought he was the King, his mind began to work again, trying to see a way out of this extraordinary situation. If, he argued to himself, he could succeed in impersonating the King, then the Germans might cease to look for him; further, if they thought they had taken him from this camp, they wouldn't come looking for gold there. Very well, so he, Rudolf Borg, was the King of Norway.

He suddenly realized that he was being asked whether he was prepared to go with them quietly—if so, he was to nod, and they would leave go of him. His decision already made, he nodded. The hand was immediately removed from his mouth and the soldiers quickly helped him to his feet and dusted the snow from his clothes. He drew himself up to his full immense height, and addressed them in a courteous voice.

"Well, gentlemen," he said, "we appear to be four against one. Kindly be good enough to inform me what your plans are with regard to my person."

"M-Major Holst has made arrangements for your reception, Your Majesty," stammered one. Holst indeed! . . . How had he managed to get here?

"Where is your Major?" he inquired.

"About half a mile away, sir. I'm afraid you'll have to walk."

Half a mile, that wasn't far. It might be a little time before he was missed, after which, of course, Captain Olsen would have no difficulty in following his tracks. The tracks, he would guess, would lead to enemy troops of some kind, and the captain would need time to make his plans, if his attack were to be a success. Idly he drew a swastika in the snow with the heel of his boot. Then he shrugged.

"I am an old man," he said, "and unaccustomed to walking. However we shall proceed."

Accompanied by his guards, he set out at a slow shuffle, his every movement watched by Astrup, only a few yards away from him.

When Carl Ringe heard what had happened, he stammered out the news to Johan.

"Rudolf Borg, indeed! Well, that figures," said Johan bitterly, and, noticing Carl's astonishment, he added, "We have Bengt Hvaldal here to thank for that. He's just told me some Germans came to Trollheim during the night and asked where the gold was hidden. They had searched the train, and found it empty. Hvaldal brightly told them we hadn't got the gold, but were escorting the King; he had to say something, or they would have shot some hostages. He's just skied out to warn us; it was a good idea, and probably would have worked," he added, "if you lot hadn't given us away by making such a bloody row. Poor old Borg. To a stranger, he certainly would resemble the King, but if they're allowed to get him back to their officer, he'll know they've got the wrong man at once. And then he'll get the truth out of him—they're bound to. He's too old to stand up to torture."

"I'm afraid you're right," said Hvaldal grimly. "Major Holst is nobody's fool."

Johan swung round on him so suddenly that Hvaldal feared he was going to be hit. "*Holst!*" he exclaimed. "Did you say Holst?"

"Yes, sir. He said that was his name. But why——?"

"How the devil did Holst get here from Dovre, on a night like this?"

"They came by car, sir. Four cars; twenty-four men in all."

"Then we outnumber them." He thought for a moment. "They must be sheltering somewhere," he said briskly. "And they won't be far off, or they couldn't have seen Borg. You local chaps, where would you say they are?"

"There's only one cabin within miles of this place," spoke up one man. "It's just on the corner as you turn off for this camp. About half a mile away."

The others nodded agreement.

"Then we'll take it that that's where they are," said Johan, "and to have seen Borg so clearly, they must be using binoculars. So we'll have to watch out. . . . If we kill this lot—every single one of them—we'll be able to join the Fifth Division tomorrow. You see, Holst is the man we've been trying to dodge—he's been on to us for the past twenty-four hours."

"Sir," interrupted Hvaldal, "we could surround that hut. There are thirty of us from Trollheim—thirty-one, counting me. We could ski round in a wide circle, and close in on them and finish them off for you."

Johan looked them over. "It could work," he said, "but we can't take any risks on Holst meeting Borg face to face. At best, he'd kill him; at worst he'd not only find out all about us from him, but he could escape and contact Oslo. If you attack their hut, I'll see about getting my Sergeant back."

"But how, sir?" asked Carl anxiously.

"I'll put on that Gestapo officer's uniform and go after him on skis, but I *must* reach him before they get him back to Holst. He'll be watching through binoculars so I'll have to make it look good. I'll take some men, of course, to cover me from the woods, but it would look better if I were alone; then they wouldn't suspect anything. Schwartz, go and find out the latest on the Borg situation."

Schwartz returned with a very breathless Krefting, who had just been across to Astrup to ask how the Sergeant was getting on.

"Shuffling, is he?" commented Johan in some amusement. "The old boy's doing his best to give us a chance to get organized. And a swastika in the snow! Well, he's certainly got his wits about him. I just hope he doesn't get rumbled too soon. . . . Listen, you men, if you're going to destroy that lot over there, you'll need some hand-grenades; rifles won't be enough for the job and, whatever you do, for Christ's sake don't shoot *me*!"

They vanished silently into the forest on skis, carrying some hand-grenades from the team's stores, and Johan turned to the team. "Now then," he said, picking up the Gestapo officer's cap and struggling into the overcoat, "I'm off to fetch Borg back. Schwartz, Krefting and Astrup, get some skis on and follow me, but keep among the trees. Don't shoot unless something goes badly wrong; those Trollheim men must be given time to get into position before any shooting starts."

"Sir," said Knut Lerdal, as Johan was strapping on his skis, "you shouldn't be completely alone."

"Why not? They won't dare to attack me. And if I'm alone, it's obvious I'm not looking for a fight."

"But it wouldn't *look* right, sir," persisted Knut. "Gestapo officers simply *don't* wander about alone in the forest at night!"

Johan weighed this point. "Very well, Lerdal," he said, "you may accompany me."

Knut nodded briefly, put on a German helmet and overcoat, and fetched a submachine-gun for himself and the Gestapo officer's Lüger for Johan.

"Now, Knut," said Johan, "listen carefully. The only dangerous part of our trip will be the very first moment. As soon as they see our uniforms they won't shoot, but we must get through the door and into the moonlight on the double. Understood? Keep that machine-gun at the ready and your wits about you and follow me. . . . Eriksen, open the door for us, and close it behind us immediately. Now!"

The two of them walked boldly out into the moonlight. After the first few steps, they realized they were over the worst hurdle.

Through his binoculars, Major Holst was watching anxiously as his men returned with 'His Majesty' at a snail's pace. "Schultz," he snapped, "we should all have attacked together. Someone's going to come out of there at any moment looking for the King, and we'll have lost the element of surprise."

Although now well out of sight of the other camp, he realized that they must be leaving tracks in the snow that could be followed without difficulty even by men on skis; the moment the King was missed, his guards would be after him like bees out of a hive. And a fight in the open against first-class marksmen was the last thing that Holst wanted.

"Let's have a look," said Schultz nervously. The binoculars changed hands just as Johan and Knut walked out into the moonlight. "Gestapo!" he breathed. "By God, sir, it's damned lucky we *didn't* attack!"

When Holst saw the Gestapo officers, he felt sick with rage. "I'm going to fetch the King myself," he announced, starting to strap on a pair of skis.

"But, sir, that man won't part with him!"

"Oh yes, I think he will. Particularly when he sees who he has to deal with! If he refuses to give in gracefully, I'll shoot him. I've got four men up there already, and he's only got one."

Schultz knew it was no use reasoning with the major when he was in that mood. He focused his binoculars on the Gestapo officer, and let Holst go without another word. But he was quite clear in his own mind that this time the Major had definitely gone too far. Deliberately to force a confrontation with the Gestapo was madness, and he for one planned to have nothing to do with it. Unnoticed by anyone, Schultz slipped behind a tree, and then, keeping carefully hidden from his companions, he moved deeper into the forest. After a harrowing trek through deep snowdrifts, with the help of neither skis nor snow-shoes, he arrived with relief at the sleeping village of Trollheim. He made his way to the station, climbed thankfully back into one of their own cars and drove back in the direction of Dovre, to rejoin the few Germans left there and make his report in whatever way appeared most advantageous to himself.

The four German soldiers holding Rudolf Borg were astonished to see a Gestapo officer approaching them on skis, and when he angrily demanded the return of his royal prisoner they looked extremely sheepish. Knut Lerdal, feeling himself into the part, bawled at them to stand to attention. Borg viewed the proceedings with an expression of mild disdain.

Johan walked over to him at once and saluted. "Your Majesty," he said, "I apologize for the indignity to which you have been subjected. If——" And then he saw a lone skier coming from the direction of the Germans' cabin; it wasn't long before he identified him as a German officer. The men from Trollheim saw him, too, but they let him go; they were not yet in position and thought it best to keep quiet—the Captain and his guards, they assumed, could handle him. And now Johan saw that this was a major—he guessed it must be Major Holst. It had not occurred to him that Holst would ski unguarded through the forest, and he had not planned on meeting him face to face; however, he stood his ground with an appearance of nonchalance, Knut Lerdal vigilant behind him. The four German soldiers watched the arrival of their officer with relief. Holst brought himself to a standstill with a neatly executed turn, faced his opponent and bowed stiffly.

"Major Heinrich Holst," he announced haughtily.

"Good evening, Major," said Johan. "An unfortunate misunderstanding. Since your men do not appear to have injured the King, I won't hold it against you, but I would be glad if you would instruct them to return my prisoner to me immediately."

Something in the tone and quality of the voice set a warning bell ringing in the Major's head; when had he heard it before? He couldn't remember; he just felt sure it had been in unfortunate circumstances. But he had set his heart on escorting the King to Oslo, and was past listening to warnings.

"The King is inadequately guarded," he said harshly, "or he would never have been allowed to walk about alone. I have twenty-four men with me, and I have come from Dovre to take him to safety, on the express orders of General von Falkenhorst. The Gestapo have other duties. You will therefore be good enough to relinquish him to me."

"My good Major, you must be joking," said Johan. "What possible reason could I have for handing my prisoner over to you?"

Something suddenly clicked in Holst's brain. Now he had it! He knew exactly where he had heard that voice before. No one had addressed Major Heinrich Holst impertinently for some considerable time; the punishment for such temerity was known to be immediate and unpleasant. No one, that is, until this very day, from Dombas station on the telephone! . . . This young upstart before him was the same man, he was quite sure of it—the man who had killed Richter. . . . So he couldn't be a German; he must be a Norwegian. . . . The moment suspicion gave way to certainty, Holst drew his pistol, but Knut, unnoticed in the background, reacted immediately. With one burst of machine-gun fire he killed Holst, then turned slightly and mowed down the four soldiers who were standing to attention in a row. Directly afterwards, shooting broke out from the direction of the Germans' cabin; the men from Trollheim had evidently taken Knut's firing as a signal to attack.

"Down!" shouted Johan, and he and Knut flattened themselves at once.

But Borg still hadn't moved; they each put up a hand and pulled him to the ground. And then he began speaking in

German. He told Johan in frigid tones that a squabble between officers in front of their men would be unheard-of in any civilized army.

"Wake up, Sergeant!" whispered Knut. "You're all right now—this is Captain Olsen, in disguise!"

"Oh, God," muttered Borg, in Norwegian, and collapsed in a heap in the snow.

A couple of rifle bullets sang past them, too close for comfort, and then Schwartz, Astrup and Krefting joined them. "If everything's okay we should go back, sir," said Schwartz, "unless we're going to join in."

"We have other responsibilities," said Johan. "We'll go back. But take charge of Mr Borg, lads; he's not feeling very well."

Johan himself felt pretty sure the old man had had a slight stroke, but he preferred to keep his opinion to himself.

Their return to the camp was greeted with tremendous relief by the others, but the shouts and congratulations were quickly put to an end by Carl Ringe. They had suffered enough that night from noisy exuberance. Johan was completely taken up with the Sergeant, who had begun to shiver violently due to a combination of cold, fatigue and nervous reaction. Only when he had seen him safely settled in a chair by the fire, muffled in blankets and with a bottle of schnapps in his hand, was he prepared to answer any of Carl's questions. Yes, it was Knut Lerdal they had heard shooting. And, yes, he had killed all four of the soldiers. Further, an officer had skied over to protest, and Knut had shot him, too. . . . And, best of all, the officer had been Major Holst himself. So now, unless they had the most appalling luck, they stood a really good chance of getting through.

Johan glanced across at Borg, and walked over to him, relieved to see him looking so much better. "Old man," he said, "I was worried about you. Now that you've recovered your spirits I want to ask you a question: I'd very much like to know what you were doing wandering about in the moonlight in the first place!"

"Would you now?" said Borg, grinning, his voice slightly slurred. Johan realized that the bottle in his hand was already more than half empty. He was glad only that the old man was in good spirits, and that his unfortunate experience did not seem to have done him any permanent damage.

Sergeant Borg closed his eyes then and in a few moments was asleep; Johan, smiling good-humouredly, carefully removed the bottle from his hand. Then he walked across to Rolf and Olaf, who were peering steadily out through a chink in one of the shutters, to ask how the fighting was going. "Still in top gear, sir," reported Olaf. "No one's come this way yet."

He remained beside them; while shooting and explosions continued there was no hope of anyone coming back to report. It was another half-hour before the shooting gradually died down. Figures on skis began to appear, and they counted the group of men returning—only ten out of thirty-one. Johan opened the door and they crowded in, exhausted and frozen, but elated. The casualties among the Norwegians were high, but not as high as had at first appeared: they had lost eleven men—the remaining ten were still in the woods searching for any Germans who might have escaped the net.

Among the casualties was Bengt Hvaldal: tired-out and over-anxious, he had blown himself up with his own hand-grenade.

The remaining men returned shortly afterwards to confirm that there was no sign of any German survivors.

A typical Norwegian
mountain road

Road through the
Dovre Mountains

The Jotenheim
Mountains

Andalsnes, looking towards the Romsdalshorn

Molde Fjord by Andalsnes, with Romsdalshorn in the background

Molde

TWELVE

BY LORRY OVER THE MOUNTAINS

JOHAN AWAKENED from a deep sleep. He opened his eyes, and saw Olaf Larsen. "You've had five hours' sleep, sir," he said. "Carl Ringe would have left you to sleep longer, but the captain of the Trollheim rifle club's been here for ages, and——"

"What's the time?"

"Ten o'clock."

"Christ, it can't be!... How's Sergeant Borg?"

"Still asleep."

"Ah, well," said Johan tolerantly, "he had a lot to celebrate last night, and he certainly did it in style. For half an hour he was the King of Norway!"

As he sipped his coffee, Carl Ringe brought a stranger over to him, whom he introduced as Aage Hansen, captain of the Trollheim rifle club. The old man sat down on the floor beside Johan.

"Rough night last night," he observed in a composed voice, as though he were referring to the weather.

"Yes," agreed Johan. "But no worse than usual."

"I gather you'd like an escort to the Fifth Division. How many men do you need?"

"About a dozen, if possible—that makes two men to each vehicle. Once we're up there, your lot could ski home again."

"I can arrange that easily. How soon do you want to start?"

"I don't like travelling by day," said Johan automatically.

"I appreciate that, but you may have to. The main road from Andalsnes to Dombas, and from there north up towards Stören, is jam-packed with allied vehicles today. And the Germans are strafing them. The allies have got air-cover and anti-aircraft guns, but you wouldn't want to join that convoy, not with the bullion. The first vehicles have just begun to turn

K

north at Dombas, but more troopships are coming into Molde. That road could be blocked all night. Of course, you could stay another night here——"

"I can't hang about. I've got to get this stuff shipped. If transports are coming in, they'll be going out again. . . . Is there any sort of mountain road to Andalsnes? I might go straight there and take cover with the Fourth Division, but I couldn't go down by the main road if it's crammed with troop transports."

Hansen shook his head; General Ruge had already warned Johan that there was no road to the ports through the mountains.

"The other way then? Towards Stören?"

"There is a mountain road from here, going east, which joins the main road somewhere between Hjerkinn and Stören. It's pretty rough and winding, but these lorries can manage it all right. I'm told that less than half the allied troops are to go north—the bulk of them are being sent to reinforce Dombas. So if you were to drive to the road junction by daylight, you could take cover and wait till you got a clear run north as far as the rearguard of the Fifth Division."

Johan pondered; he would prefer to start at dusk, and he said so.

"It would be suicide! If you'd seen the mountain road, you'd understand what I mean; no one would risk a road like that in the dark, and if you used headlights you'd be visible from one end of the Gudbrands Valley to the other!"

"Well, thanks for the information, and the offer of extra men. Perhaps you'd give us a little while to talk it over."

Shortly before twelve o'clock, Hansen returned, and Johan noticed at once that he had far more than a dozen men with him—it looked like nearer twenty. Hansen, waving a freshly lighted cigar, explained the position. "These extra men," he said, "insisted on coming. So I let them. I thought you wouldn't mind. . . . And I'm coming myself. We've all brought our rifles and food for ourselves, and some fresh food for you, and plenty of petrol. And the white tarpaulins from the train, to help camouflage the lorries."

Johan thought it would be ungracious to refuse the extra help, so he told them they were all very welcome.

The convoy started off, with two drivers in each lorry and the extra men travelling among the crates of bullion under the tarpaulins. Johan drove the leading lorry, with Olaf beside him, Carl Ringe with Eriksen brought up the rear, and Aage Hansen and Rudolf Borg were somewhere in the middle.

The road wound its way up and up and up as it mounted the first ridge of the foothills of the Dovre Heights; they were above the tree-line when they reached the first crest, and began to descend into the valley. The lorries, strung out in a long line as they circled downwards, could not fail to be visible for miles in every direction, in spite of the partial camouflage, but, as Hansen had said, the full attention of the enemy was at the moment focused on the unbroken column of troop transports driving up the main road to Dombas. Planes could be heard from time to time, and seen.

At long last the track straightened out as it entered its final stretch before the junction with the main road, and Johan gathered speed. Soon one of the local men allotted to his lorry crept over the stacked crates and shouted in Johan's ear that the main road was round the next corner. He decided to pull in to the side of the road and halt where they were, and send someone to scout ahead and report back whether the road was clear. Now that they had crossed the mountains and were back on level ground again, there was no fear that the engines would freeze as long as the sun continued to shine brightly.

One by one the lorries came round the last corner, and parked behind the leader—all twelve of them, Johan noticed with satisfaction. The men began to jump to the ground; he told them sharply to keep off the road, and exercise in the woods.

After a while the messenger returned with the disappointing news that the main road was still blocked by a solid mass of crawling vehicles; they would have to wait. A permanent guard was left on the corner to report immediately any slackening in the traffic, and at about five o'clock Johan heard with relief that the allied convoy had come to an abrupt end. They all quickly returned to their lorries and started up again. No one knew how far north the Fifth Division rearguard would be, and they did not want to have to use headlights.

The main road proved a great disappointment to the team. Although much wider than the mountain track, it was almost as precipitous; they had been expecting a clear run up. Suddenly, without warning, the second-last lorry, manned by Rolf Bergstrom and Ivor Astrup, failed to make the crest of a hill. The engine puttered out, and clouds of steam poured out of the radiator.

Carl Ringe, behind them with Eriksen, pulled out and passed them, only stopping when he had successfully topped the rise, in case the same thing should happen to his own lorry. Leaving the engine running, they walked back.

"Take the brake off and back her down a bit and have another shot," suggested Carl. It was useless. "Eriksen, get your skis on at once, and go and tell the Captain. Be as quick as you can—you must catch up with him while they're all going downhill; you can't stop them once they've started climbing the next gradient."

Eriksen reached the leading lorry well before it started to climb again, passed it, fetched up in the middle of the road, and waved. Olaf stopped, and Johan leant over the side.

Eriksen told him what had happened, and Johan turned to Olaf. "D'you think you'd be able to fix it?" he asked.

"I can but try! If I can't get her going at all, what shall I do?"

"We'll send some men back to look for you as soon as we reach the army. Tell them you're 'Fridtjof'—that should be sufficient. And take all the spare men back with you off the other lorries as you go past—you may need them. Eriksen, wait here for Ringe; he'll pick you up as he goes past."

Johan started up again, with a local man sitting beside him. When Carl saw Olaf coming up, and the other lorries moving on, he got into his own lorry and followed on, encouraged by urgent signals from Eriksen, stranded at the side of the road.

Olaf reached the broken-down lorry with about ten men. He opened the bonnet immediately, and started to try to trace the fault; the daylight was already fading.

Meanwhile the rest of the convoy continued. They topped the next two crests and negotiated two more winding valleys when suddenly the road in front of him was alive with men in white coats. A Second Lieutenant approached him, and asked who he was.

" 'Fridtjof' " replied Johan.

"Fridtjof? Fridtjof who?"

"Go and fetch the nearest senior officer at once," snapped Johan.

As he spoke he saw a Colonel walking towards him. With relief he recognized him; it was Kaare Pedersen.

"Well, Johan," he called cheerfully, "so *you're* 'Fridtjof'! You're just in time; Colonel Hagen's been here for two hours, hoping you'd show up. He says there are no telephones working at Andalsnes, and you hadn't sent a message to us. He was just leaving—I'll fetch him at once. The allies went straight through, and left us at the rear for a few hours' rest."

As he was speaking, a staff car started to drive down the road towards them; Colonel Pedersen stopped it, and came back with Colonel Hagen. "You've just caught me," he said. "I would have been sorry to miss you—I came up to try to make some arrangements with you. We've no phones at Andalsnes, or any water, I'm afraid—Fourth Division started where the Germans left off, and they've been through the town like a dose of salts, clearing out paratroopers; the town's still burning. But I've got two destroyers who have volunteered to come in for the gold reserves. They'll each take a third—orders are to spread the risk. We'll see about the rest as soon as possible. Can you come on down tonight?"

"One of my lorries is adrift, I'm afraid," Johan told him. "It broke down a few miles back. I'll have to wait for it—it's carrying seven tons of bullion."

Hagen considered. "That could take till dawn," he said, "and you won't want to travel by daylight. . . . Come on down tomorrow night, and I'll send for the destroyers on the next evening tide. They're cruising off Molde; nothing can wait in either harbour for long—it's too risky. I'll get back to Andalsnes now and send a signal to Molde. When can we expect you?"

"I'll leave here at dusk tomorrow."

"Very well. You could make Andalsnes in about four hours from here, I should think. We'll be on the lookout for you, and I'll have thought out a place to hide those lorries before you arrive. The German bombers pay us a visit every day, but luckily more or less at the same time—about dawn. I imagine it's just to stop us using the port, because there's really nothing left to destroy."

"Wouldn't it be better, then, sir, if I were to drive straight on to Molde?"

"No. For one thing, it's a physical impossibility—you can only get to Molde by ferry. That would expose those lorries to quite a long sea-voyage, and nobody likes the thought of that. And the King and his party are being taken off from Molde; we can't have you all waiting in the same place. The British cruiser *Glasgow* is coming in for him; at the moment, she's somewhere on the high seas. Also, the enemy aren't expecting us to use Andalsnes any more, so it's the best place for you, really."

"Where is His Majesty, sir?"

"He's at Afarnes. It's so small that the enemy have ignored it so far. The royal party and the government took the passenger ferry from Andalsnes to Afarnes, and as soon as the *Glasgow*'s ready to come alongside at Molde they'll take another ferry from Afarnes to Molde. By the way, I've arranged for you to use your code-name if you're challenged at Dombas. The allies don't know what you're carrying, but they have orders to escort you straight through. I wonder if there's anything else. . . ." He thought for a moment. "Ah, yes, dockyard passes. I've left some for you with Pedersen—he'll fix you up. They're absolutely essential, so don't forget them. Ask for me personally when you arrive."

As soon as he had gone, Pedersen came over to Johan. "Let's get your stuff stashed," he said, "and I'll send some men back at once to find your lost lorry. How many men are guarding it?"

"About fifteen. We borrowed extra men for this journey, and I left most of them behind to guard it. Local riflemen."

"Well, then, there shouldn't be too much to worry about. I'll send a messenger over to tell you as soon as it's located."

"What was that that Hagen said about passes for the dockyard?"

"Oh, just an idea of his own. They've got parachutists on the brain down there, and no wonder. The passes are just scraps of paper, really, signed by Hagen himself. I'll give them to you in the morning."

THIRTEEN

ATTACK BY WOLVES

IT DID NOT TAKE Olaf Larsen more than a few moments to find out why the lorry had broken down; the fan-belt, although it had not snapped, was stretched and useless. It was beginning to get dark, and if he didn't get the engine going soon it would freeze.

"You could try once more, Astrup," he said hopefully, "now that she's cool. She might just get you over the crest, and then we'd be able to freewheel downhill for a few miles before she stopped again."

Astrup tried, but he had backed the lorry quite a long way down the hill on Carl Ringe's instructions, and before he reached the top she was boiling again, and had cut out.

"Well, we can't push her," said Olaf. "Not with that load."

"We passed a track a short way back," observed one of their guards. "Tracks always lead somewhere."

"That's true," said Olaf, "and every place up here will have a vehicle of some kind—let's just hope it's the right kind! . . . Astrup, stay here with the lorry. Rolf and I will ski up there and try to get a fan-belt."

Half a mile down the track they reached a log-cabin with outbuildings; they were just coming up to the front door when suddenly Olaf turned aside and skied into the woods, signalling to Rolf to follow him.

"What's the matter?" panted Rolf. "Did you imagine you saw a German helmet?"

"No! But I just thought it might be wiser not to ask permission after all. The owner might refuse to part with his fan-belt. And we can't explain to all and sundry that we're stranded with seven tons of gold bullion! So I'm afraid I'm going to have to pop round and pinch one. You stay here with my skis. I'll be back in a moment."

Rolf, listening apprehensively, was most relieved when Olaf

came running back. "Here, take this!" he panted, throwing the fan-belt at Rolf and strapping on his skis. "Let's go!"

"Are you sure it'll fit?"

"I'm sure it won't! But we can stretch it. It should take us a few miles at least. And then we might be lucky enough to find someone else with a lorry."

Astrup and one of the old men together managed to get the fan-belt fitted. He put her into gear again and she took the hill like a bird. As they neared the next crest, they were all praying that she would make it—and so she did, but only just. The fan-belt broke with a snap, and Astrup said to Olaf, "Well, at least we made about five miles! Not bad. But we don't want to stop up here—it's freezing. . . . Listen, you men," he said, turning round, "I'm going to freewheel her down into the valley slowly, and I want everyone to keep their eyes skinned for a track leading off as we go. I should think it would be best to stop for the night if we find anywhere suitable. Captain Olsen said he'd send someone back to look for us, and they'll be bound to find our tracks."

At the bottom of the valley, several of the men called excitedly that there was a track leading off to the right; there was still just enough light to make out the break in the trees. Astrup pulled into the side of the road.

"Rolf and I will ski down there and see what's at the other end," said Olaf. "There'll probably be a lorry."

Suddenly two men stepped out of the trees. "Good evening," said the elder. "We didn't think that fan-belt would get you this far!"

"Are you from the Fifth Division?" asked Olaf eagerly.

"No. We live here."

"But—but you were expecting us," stammered Olaf. "Who told you anything about us?"

"My grandfather!" said the younger one. "He telephoned us. As soon as he told us what belt you'd taken, we knew it wouldn't fit that lorry. As my father just said, everyone expected you to break down before you topped that last crest—there were men along the road waiting to help you back there."

"What's going on?" demanded Astrup. "How the devil did anyone know we were coming?"

The forester laughed. "All the farmers and foresters from Trollheim to Stören were warned to keep an eye on you. Aage Hansen passed the message on early this morning, in case any of the lorries should need help."

"He had no right to telephone! Captain Olsen would be furious."

"Hansen wasn't born yesterday. He didn't use any telephone. He just told someone to ski to the nearest farm and pass the message right up the line. It didn't take long. So everyone counted twelve lorries as they passed, and then suddenly there were only eleven. Got it? Well, now, I expect you're all cold and hungry, so we'd better get you settled down for the night. I wonder if that lorry's up to driving down our track?"

But this time there was no chance of getting her to go another inch; the radiator had burst.

"Well," said the elder of the two men, "take the brake off and steer it among the trees—you're facing downhill."

With the lorry hidden, they no longer felt too worried. "We'll offload the bullion and take it up to our place on sledges," said the forester. "That would be the quickest job. How much is there?"

"Seven tons."

"Jesus! . . . Well, we'd better get cracking then, or it'll take all night. We've got four sledges; how many men have you got?"

"About fifteen. Captain Olsen left us all the spares."

"We'll fetch the sledges and get on with it."

"Astrup," said Olaf, "you go on up with them. Rolf and I will stay here by the roadside to guard the bullion."

It was nearly two hours before the last of the crates had been unloaded and stacked by the roadside. The moon had risen by this time, and was shining from a clear, starry sky, and the two boys realized how conspicuous they would be if anyone should pass that way.

"Olaf," said Rolf nervously, after a while, "I feel as though we are being watched."

"I expect we are," said Olaf, in as cheerful a voice as he could manage, "by some inquisitive forest trolls! Keep quiet, and we might be lucky enough to see one."

Olaf's remark had been made to calm Rolf's nerves, but as they both stood motionless he suddenly became conscious of the same instinctive awareness that had possessed Rolf—they *were* being watched. Or were they? He shrugged. Imagination, probably. And then from the top of the cliff came a faint suppressed howl, repeated twice on a more confident note. Olaf felt a prickly sensation down his spine; wolves. So Rolf had been right. "We'll let off our rifles," he whispered nervously. "That's the way to scare off wolves."

"No!" snapped Rolf. "Wolves wouldn't come down into the foothills—you know they wouldn't. It's *Harald*, that's who it is; it's his danger signal. He must have come to warn us that something's gone wrong. I'll climb up and talk to him; you wait there."

Olaf was not convinced. He watched anxiously as Rolf scrambled expertly up the precipice, pulling himself up by rocks and stunted trees. And then, just as he reached the top, Olaf saw several pairs of eyes gleaming in the moonlight above him. "Rolf!" he screamed in terror. "Come down! It *is* wolves!"

But Rolf had already reached the top. As his right hand grasped a tree, he looked up, grinning, expecting to see Harald, and found himself face to face with the leader of the pack. There was a vicious snarl, a terrified scream, and Rolf, losing his balance, plummeted down to the bottom of the cliff, and lay still. The suddenness of the accident paralysed Olaf for a moment, and then he was running towards Rolf, yelling for help.

The other men, on their way back to the roadside for the umpteenth time, heard the sounds; the forester and his son automatically discharged their rifles into the air, reloaded and fired again. "All the wrong reactions," said the father irritably. "Wolves are very timid, really. A few shots always scare them off—screaming only encourages them."

No one thought at first that anything serious had happened, but as Olaf's yells continued, they all broke into a run.

Astrup was first on the scene. "What happened?" he asked Olaf. "Was Rolf attacked?"

"No, he fell off the cliff. He's unconscious. He thought the wolf was Harald calling him—he said it was a family danger signal."

"Let's have a look at him," said Astrup grimly. He examined Rolf, and then looked up at Olaf, shocked and distressed. "I'm fearfully sorry, old chap," he said. "I'm afraid he's dead!"

"Oh, Astrup, *no*!"

"Take a look for yourself, then. His neck's broken."

And then they suddenly heard the swish of several pairs of skis, and were surrounded by men flashing torches. "Lieutenant Myrseth, Fifth Division," stated a voice sharply. "Who are you?"

" 'Fridtjof'," answered Olaf mechanically.

"Good! Thank God we've found you. We couldn't see the lorry anywhere, and then we heard the rifle shots. Is the gold safe?"

"Yes," Astrup told him. "We're just putting the last of it away. Some foresters live here; we've been taking it to their cabin by sledge."

"Right. . . . Now, what's going on here? An accident?"

"Broken neck, I'm afraid," said Astrup. "He fell off the cliff. . . . He *is* dead, isn't he, Olaf?"

Olaf nodded; the tears were streaming down his face.

"Pity we couldn't have got here sooner," said the Lieutenant. "How did it happen?"

"The wolves frightened him."

"Wolves? As far down as this?"

"They come down from the mountains sometimes after a very long winter like this," the forester told him. "Poor little bastard. Let's carry him inside."

The soldiers checked that all was in order, and said they would go back and report to Colonel Pedersen and Captain Olsen at once, and then the exhausted men settled down in the warm cabin. Astrup managed to get Olaf to eat a little, and drink something, but he was in a daze of exhaustion and grief. It was a long time before he fell into an uneasy sleep, haunted by dreams of wolves, trolls and Germans in Norwegian uniform.

Three miles away, the news that the lost lorry had been found and that the gold was safe was received with great relief by the rest of the team. Tomorrow evening they would be able to drive down together to Andalsnes and say goodbye to the bullion on the following evening's tide. The only thing that disturbed them was the report that one man had been killed. Johan said that Carl should ski over there and take charge, as there was no one with any authority in that camp; the soldiers would show them where it was.

"Sir," asked Harald immediately, "may I go with Mr Ringe? It's just that I——"

"It's just that you want to make sure your brother's all right! Very well, Corporal Bergstrom, you may go."

Carl and Harald entered the warm hut out of the freezing cold, as their guides skied thankfully back to their own camp, promising to send an army lorry down for the bullion in the morning. It was dark and everyone was asleep, but they were both anxious to check up on Rolf, Olaf and Astrup. Carl lit the paraffin lamp; the men stirred in their sleep and woke up gradually at the sound of heavy boots tramping round the room.

Carl went over to speak to Astrup; Olaf, tossing and turning on the floor, was jerked to full consciousness by the toe of a boot in the small of his back. He opened his eyes, and saw Harald Bergstrom glaring down at him. "Olaf," he said sharply, "I can't find Rolf. Where is he?"

Olaf's eyes filled with tears; the sudden appearance of Harald was the last straw. Harald's throat tightened when he saw Olaf's woebegone face; surely to God he can't have lost both the twins in two days? "Olaf, answer me!" he ordered, his voice sharp with anxiety. "Where is Rolf?"

"I'm terribly sorry, Harald," whispered Olaf, "he's dead!"

"But what happened? Everyone else looks all right. What happened to Rolf?"

Olaf was silent, trying to think of words to explain how Rolf had died without causing his brother more pain than he already had to endure.

And then the old man lying next to him spoke up. "Larking about at the cliff-face, they were, Corporal, the pair of them," he said. "Then one of them got a fright and fell off."

"My God, young Larsen," growled Harald menacingly, "I'll make you pay for this! You were the elder. . . ."

"Go easy on him, Corporal," put in the same man. "He's terribly upset."

"Upset!" roared Harald. "My brother's *dead*!"

His brother. . . . The old man realized that by speaking he had only made things much worse. Harald had one huge arm round Olaf's neck, practically strangling him, and then his eyes began searching round the room. He was obviously look-ing for a weapon, and appeared quite oblivious to his surround-ings. Suddenly he saw a large poker lying by the fireside; dragging Olaf with him, he crossed the room and seized it. "And now, young Larsen," he snarled, "you're going to see what happens to little boys who lark about and get their friends killed. . . !"

Carl Ringe, who, like the others, had been watching Harald's behaviour in appalled silence, stepped forward at once.

"Bergstrom!" he called sharply.

"You keep out of this, you jumped-up, sodding great bastard!" roared Harald.

Carl hesitated fractionally, then caught Astrup's eye and nodded. The next second, Harald found himself flying across the room; he hit the wall and fell heavily, while the poker clattered to the ground. Clutching a damaged wrist, Harald looked up at Astrup, who was standing over him, panting, and then across at Carl.

"All right, all right," he growled. "You can call your dog off. But that boy deserves a whipping, and you know it as well as I do."

"He does not!" It was Astrup who had spoken up. "If Olaf won't tell you why Rolf died, I will, and let's have an end of this. He thought the wolf was *you* calling him—he said it was a family danger signal. But of all the darnfool, crazy signals to choose, the call of a hunting wolf!"

Harald had gone quite white. He got shakily to his feet, and then forced himself to look across at Olaf.

"Olaf," he whispered, "is that true?"

"Yes, Harald, I'm afraid it is. I wanted to spare you. . . ."

Harald glanced round the circle of anxious faces with the expression of a wounded animal; then he backed through the kitchen door and slammed it shut, and in the dead silence which followed they all listened helplessly to his bitter, heart-broken sobbing.

"For Christ's sake," said the forester to his son, "go and give that poor devil a bottle of something—a full bottle. And then we can all get a bit of sleep."

FOURTEEN

THE STRICKEN PORT OF ANDALSNES

IT WAS ELEVEN O'CLOCK the following morning. An army lorry had called at dawn and brought Carl, Olaf, Harald and Astrup and the missing bullion to their proper destination, the Trollheim men had gone home, and now everyone was waiting for dusk, when they would start on the final leg of their journey to Andalsnes. Ringe and Borg were in earnest conversation in one corner of the room, and Olaf, Emil, Knut and Theodor Storm in another; they were anxiously awaiting the Captain's decision as to what was going to happen to Harald Bergstrom. He had been closeted with the Captain and Colonel Pedersen ever since Carl Ringe had made his report on the events of the previous night.

At last they heard the scraping of chairs in the next room. Olaf, unable to bear the suspense any longer, jumped up, went and opened the door and stood uncertainly in the doorway. Harald's corporal's stripes were lying on the table, and he was looking white and strained. Olaf, embarrassed, avoided his eyes.

"Come in, Larsen," said the Captain, "and shut the door."

Olaf looked at the stripes, and then questioningly up at Captain Olsen. Johan shrugged. "This is an extremely distressing matter," he said. "The fact that our only two casualties so far should have been Bergstrom's brothers is the worst possible bad luck, and he has my deepest sympathy, but after his appalling behaviour last night he obviously can't continue as a member of the team. He fully understands—and you must understand also—that our first duty is to the gold bullion, and, through no fault of his own, Harald can no longer be regarded as reliable. I suggested that he should join the Fifth Division as an ordinary soldier, and he has agreed to do so. He's leaving now, with Colonel Pedersen."

He held out his hand to Harald, who took it shyly. "Good

luck, Bergstrom," he said. "You've been a very valuable member of the team up till now, and you may be sure that I shall say so in my report."

He paused. Harald was looking across at Olaf. "Olaf," he said, rather uncertainly, "will you—will you shake hands?"

For answer, Olaf was across the room in an instant, and hurling himself into Harald's arms. "There now," said Harald, rather huskily. "We'll all meet again when this is over, won't we?"

"Yes, Harald. And—and good luck."

As the two of them walked across to the Colonel's car, Pedersen suddenly turned round. "Johan," he said, "this means that you're short three men—I'll send replacements. What type of men do you want?"

"Level-headed, as I said," said Johan, "and good drivers. But for God's sake make sure they're not related to each other!"

Johan had one more matter to settle before he himself could rest.

"Larsen," he called, "come back in here for a moment. I want to talk to you." When he had closed the door again, he said, "The departure of Bergstrom leaves Sergeant Borg without a corporal." He picked up Harald's stripes, and gave them to him. "You are now the Corporal of that watch," he said. "Do your best."

"*Me*, sir? But I've had no military training!"

"I know that. But as the team's mechanic you should have some authority. Also, you've proved yourself extremely reliable in every way. No, don't argue. It's for me to decide."

The three replacements appeared about an hour later, on skis. Looking for someone to report to, they encountered what appeared to be a bunch of terrifying gangsters. Startled, they drew together like frightened sheep. The team eyed the 'new boys' with sardonic amusement.

"Well, what have we here?" asked Eriksen, grinning rather maliciously. "You wouldn't have any names, I suppose, would you?"

It turned out that by a coincidence two of the men were christened Björn and the surname of the third was Björnsen. Inevitably Eriksen nicknamed them the 'Three Bears'.

L

Olaf scowled at them. To him they were a bunch of inter-
lopers who had come to take the place of the Bergstroms.
"Well," he said, "I'll just go and check my lorries. We don't
want any more breakdowns."

"May I help you, Corporal?" asked one of the 'Bears'
bravely.

"Do you know anything about engines?" growled Olaf.

"Yes, Corporal. I'm a garage mechanic." The man stood
smartly to attention, rather wishing he'd kept his mouth shut.

"Oh, really?" The others grinned at Olaf's embarrassment;
he had had no experience of people standing to attention
when they spoke to him. "Well, come along then," he said.
"I could do with some help."

As they walked out, he asked, "Have you people been told
what we're carrying?"

"Oh, yes, Corporal!" was the enthusiastic reply.

"Well, then, let's get to work."

In discussing the engines and checking them with someone
who understood them as well as he did himself, Olaf's bruised
spirits began to recover; tomorrow their mission would be
completed, and they could all join Harald and take the chance
of doing a bit of fighting with the army before going underground.

The team were looking forward tremendously to this final
stage. They borrowed extra drivers from the army, and the
convoy got under way at about seven o'clock. Johan had
expected to be held up for some time at Dombas, but the
town was still firmly in the hands of the allies, and when he
gave his code-name, as Pedersen had arranged for him to do,
he was escorted straight through at once.

They reached Andalsnes at about midnight. The lorries
were silhouetted by the dull glow of many fires, and here, if
anywhere, in the stricken town itself, Johan feared that they
might be attacked. He gathered speed, and confidently approached the dockyard gates, but was annoyed to find them
locked. He had expected that Colonel Hagen would have
alerted the guard, but he was not even challenged. He climbed
out of the lorry, stiff and cold, and found himself surrounded
by about twenty marines.

"Your pass, please," demanded a Sergeant.

He produced a handful of yellow cards that Colonel Pedersen had given him from Colonel Hagen.

"There are no names on these. Where did you get them?"

"Colonel Hagen gave them to me. And we don't want to hang about. Please fetch him at once."

At that moment a Lieutenant appeared, "Good evening," said Johan, with relief. "I'm Captain Olsen. I'm sorry we didn't fill in Colonel Hagen's passes—I didn't have time to look at them, actually! I'll show you my personal papers if you like."

"Put your hands up!" The command was so sharp that Johan obeyed instinctively. "I'll get your papers myself," said the officer of marines. He took them out of Johan's breast pocket, looked at them carefully, and then handed them back with a smile and an apology. "Colonel Hagen's told me about you, of course," he said. "All right, men, look alive! Open up those gates. We've learnt by bitter experience," he continued, "to regard all strangers as enemies down here. Germans in Norwegian uniforms are a constant menace. I was of course expecting your convoy, but I couldn't be sure who would actually arrive in it!"

The Lieutenant directed Johan across to the far side of the dockyard, until he was able to make out the dark mouth of a tunnel. He stopped. "Are we to go in there?" he asked.

"That's the idea. It's the only really safe place here. A direct hit from a bomb might come through, but they're not dropping H.E.s—only small stuff. Incendiaries mostly, actually, just to keep us on the hop. We have one air raid daily, at half past seven in the morning; the great thing is that they won't be able to see you in this tunnel."

"What goes on at the other end?" asked Johan suspiciously. "I don't want to be boxed in."

"You won't be. There are steel gates at either end, and you can have the keys. The tunnel was built so that valuable freight could be kept at the docks in safety while awaiting shipment—from a train, of course—but there's plenty of room for lorries; you can drive them in along the platforms on both sides of the track. I'll send a few goods trolleys over in the morning, for moving the gold when it's to be shipped. You can't risk driving the lorries down to the quay—a reconnaissance plane could easily spot you."

"Well, thanks very much. This looks perfect."

"The hideout's perfect, yes, but that's about all! Otherwise, the port's a complete shambles. Now, don't forget to give each man a pass, with his name and signature on it; the passes are to be shown with their military papers whenever they're challenged."

"My men don't have any papers. There wasn't time."

"Tell Colonel Hagen in the morning. In the meantime, I'll send some water over to you, and don't let any of the men out until their papers are in order. I mean that—they could get shot."

"I'll remember. What's your name, by the way?"

"Jensen. Per Jensen."

"Who else knows what my cargo is?"

"Colonel Hagen and the harbour-master. That's all."

"We'll keep it that way."

"That's the arrangement. . . ."

It did not take them long to get safely settled in the tunnel. They had brought two extra lorries to sleep in, and Johan put one at each end of the tunnel, with two riflemen on duty in each one. Before going to sleep himself, he tested the keys of both gates, and then locked them in.

The following morning, they were able to see for themselves that the port was in a terrible state. Every installation had been destroyed; there were gaping holes in the harbour walls and bomb-craters everywhere. The morning air raid came and went, a cursory affair which did no damage; there was simply nothing left to destroy.

The harbour-master paid a visit to the tunnel. "I came to tell you that your destroyers are dodging between the islands," he said. "We're in touch with them. I'll get a signal off to them now to confirm that they are to come in at dusk this evening."

"The port seems very deserted," observed Johan.

"Yes, it is. No more troopships are coming in here—there isn't enough air-cover for two ports, so all the troopships are using Molde now. You're my last responsibility."

The harbour-master's confirmation that their destroyers were actually in the Molde Fjord and ready to take off their cargo filled the men with a sense of relief.

The mood of exhilaration went on all day. Carl asked Johan what he planned to do tomorrow; he had not even considered the question—his whole attention had been taken up with getting his cargo successfully to Andalsnes. However, he said he supposed they would join the Fourth or Fifth Division for a while, just till the fighting ended.

"But when the fighting's ended," persisted Carl. "Couldn't we all stick together somehow?"

"I hadn't thought. We could form a resistance group of our own, I suppose," he suggested suddenly. The more he thought about the idea, the more it appealed to him. The team were delighted; they had thought for some reason that he would be going to England with the gold, to look after it.

"Once I've handed it over, that's it, as far as I'm concerned," Johan said. "I'm a soldier, not a ruddy banker!"

Towards evening, the men fell silent. Living with the gold had almost become a way of life, and they found that, now that the journey was nearly over, they were going to find it very difficult to fit back into ordinary life again.

Just before dusk Colonel Hagen came to see them, bringing a special stamp to stamp their yellow passes. He said it was the best he could do if they had no papers, and the marines had been informed of the arrangement. It would at least allow them to leave the tunnel in safety. One by one they went down to the quay.

Just before high water slack, a British destroyer came in. She was well camouflaged—Olaf was the first to spot her.

The destroyer's Captain, a Lieutenant Commander, R.N., appeared at the top of the gangway, with a Lieutenant. "Do you speak English?" he inquired anxiously.

"Yes, I do."

"Thank God for that! All I can say in Norwegian is 'I love you'."

Johan laughed. "I presume you've come to take off my gold bullion for me?"

"Indeed I have. I'll get your little lot stowed away first, and then you can come aboard for a drink. I don't want to stay long; the tide's just turning. I'd like it to take me out again. My navigating officer and the local pilot practically came to blows, though—I don't think the local man was used to bringing in such a big ship. Now lead me to the treasure."

"You should bring with you as many men as possible," Johan advised him. "The gold is heavy. We have trolleys, but very few men."

"Well, I suppose six men should be enough."

"Not unless they're giants! With forty men, it takes about two hours to load the whole consignment. I know you're taking only a part of it, but this time it'll all have to be brought to your ship for loading."

The naval officer felt it would be tactful to pretend that he believed this tall story, and good-humouredly sent for the whole of the duty-watch, and together they tramped through the snow to the tunnel. The Englishman began to count the number of seven-ton trucks stacked with crates, and then he looked at Johan with new respect.

"What's the total weight?" he asked.

"Over 80 tons."

"Suffering Christ, as much as that? . . . Well, if we're to take one third of it, it would take us at least an hour to load from this distance, even if we had a crane, and we haven't a crane. . . . Chief," he called, "go and rig up some sort of tackle to get this stuff on board."

The sailors soon improvised a workable loading system. It was well over an hour before the thirty tons or so of gold had been shipped; Carl and some of the team had been looking out anxiously for the other destroyer, but the tide had turned some time before, and there was still no sign of her.

When Johan finally went on board the English ship for a drink, her Captain offered to try and get in touch with the other destroyer for him before leaving; he sent his First Lieutenant to see whether she could be raised. He came back to the wardroom shortly. "Bad news, I'm afraid," he said. "The Johnny Frenchman's gone aground—her Captain's swearing blue murder. He doesn't even seem to know exactly where he is, so he's going to wait till dawn before proceeding. He's missed the tide."

"A French destroyer?" exclaimed Johan in dismay. "But—but where will she take my gold?"

The Englishman roared with laughter. "You don't trust her,

eh?" said the captain.

"If the gold goes to France," said Johan earnestly, "how can we get it out again? We would hand it to the Germans, as you English say, 'on a plate'. France will soon be occupied."

"You think so?"

"Indeed I do."

"Well, your gold will all go to England, don't you worry, whoever takes it out of Norway. This is a combined operation."

"I understand. Wouldn't it be possible for you to take the rest of the gold while you're here?" asked Johan hopefully. "The other ship may be damaged, and heaven knows where a third ship's to come from."

"I *could*, of course, but I'm afraid I'm not allowed to; we were told to spread the risk. A third ship will come, you'll see, and as for this French one, she won't be damaged—she would have said so."

"Well, if you're in touch with her again, please be good enough to inform her that there is an air raid every morning at half past seven."

"We'll make a point of telling her. . . . And now I only hope I get out as quickly as I came in."

"You are bound for where?"

"Scotland. We're going straight across. We should be there before morning."

"I thank you," said Johan, "on behalf of my country."

He watched the English destroyer sail away on the tide with her quota of his precious cargo; he hoped that someone might think of letting him know some time if it ever reached its destination. He told the harbour-master that the other destroyer was aground; the official said he hoped very much that she would be afloat again soon, or the Germans would see her when they came to raid the port in the morning. He told Johan he would arrange to have a few wrecked cars towed on to the dockyard during the night to distract their attention; the destroyer would be camouflaged—this was the best he could do to help her.

Johan returned to the tunnel, and broke the news to the men that the other destroyer was aground, but hoped to get refloated on the next tide.

"Sir, are you sure she'll come?" asked Knut Lerdal.

"No one can be sure of anything," said Johan irritably. "All I know is, we can't allow her to load in daylight. You saw how long the English destroyer took—it's just not on. She'll have to refloat and come in here tomorrow evening."

So they would have to spend at least another twenty-four hours here, whatever happened. . . .

"Is the other destroyer not English, sir?" asked Carl.

"No, she's French. . . . We'll hear from her soon; the harbour-master's trying to contact her. We can only hope she hasn't gone aground within sight of Andalsnes, or the German planes might see her in the morning. They're putting vehicles of some sort on the dockyard during the night—with any luck that should keep the raiders' attention from wandering. . . ."

FIFTEEN

THE DESPAIR OF ISOLATION

AT ABOUT SIX O'CLOCK in the morning, everyone was awakened by the sound of shouting and swearing from the quayside—some of the men were talking in Norwegian, and the rest in French. Johan, accompanied by Carl and the Sergeant, raced towards the quay. They were horrified to see marines with fixed bayonets barring the path of more than fifty men in dark blue uniforms who were trying to land.

"They're from our ship!" cried Carl.

"For God's sake let's prevent the marines from murdering those wretched sailors!" said Johan. "You two, you both speak French—go and find out what's going on. I'll tackle the marines."

As Johan ran up, yelling explanations in Norwegian, he saw that Hagen and Jensen were there before him, and that the menace was now coming from the angry Frenchmen—Ringe and Borg had arrived just in time. They ascertained, to everyone's dismay, that the French destroyer had gone aground in full view of the port, and the captain had decided, in view of the imminent air raid, that the only thing to do was to abandon ship. The raid, they had been told, was usually at half past seven, and it was now seven o'clock; the Captain and the other watch were still on board—the boats had gone back for them. When Borg explained that Norwegian time was different and it was only six, the whole contingent relaxed. Carl then asked where the destroyer was. Following the pointing finger of the First Lieutenant, he could at first see nothing in the way of a ship; she was certainly extremely well camouflaged, and he would not have seen her at all if he had not been told exactly where to look. However, at half past seven, when it would be much lighter, she might well be visible to a low-flying aircraft, stuck as she was on a rocky island; without air-cover, he realized that they had been right to abandon ship.

"Well, Olsen," said Hagen, "we can only hope the vehicles the harbour-master asked me to put on the dockyard last night will be sufficiently interesting to keep their eyes off that target! Do the Frenchmen know about the cars?"

Carl explained to the Lieutenant. They would know soon enough how effective it was. Hagen suggested that the Frenchmen should be hidden in the tunnel till after the raid; dark uniforms on the snow-covered dockyard would be visible for miles.

"Carl," asked Johan, "do the rest of your team speak good French?"

"Yes, all of them."

"In that case, please explain to the Lieutenant that we will escort his party to cover. You and Borg must wait here on the quay to meet the destroyer's Captain and the rest of her crew, and bring them straight over."

The French Captain, when he arrived, decided to have the ship's boats pulled ashore and covered with snow, since if they should be bombed there would be no means of returning to the ship. The whole ship's company were installed inside the tunnel by a quarter past seven. The air was suddenly filled with sound; today they had sent four planes instead of the usual two. Crouched in the tunnel, the team and their allies watched.

The Germans noticed with glee the cars which the harbour-master had laid out the evening before, and when they had reduced them all to flaming wrecks they turned to go. The French destroyer, whose camouflage fitted in perfectly with her background of water, snow and pine-trees, was not noticed. They waited for about ten minutes after the departure of the planes before venturing out of the tunnel. It was now possible to make out the outline of the destroyer where she lay beached.

Johan now began to discuss the position, in English, with the French Captain. The Frenchman had by now been told that Captain Olsen was in charge of the gold reserves, and assured him that the French were anxious to help. It would, he said, be high tide in an hour's time, when he would be able to refloat his ship. He offered to bring her alongside, take off his quota of the bullion, and let the tide take him out again.

Although Johan had already decided against loading in broad daylight, at the same time he could not lightly cast aside what might well be his last chance of getting the better part of his cargo to safety. He told the Captain of his fears, and asked him if he would consider taking cover in one of the numerous inlets along the thickly forested coastline for the day, and then returning after dusk and taking the gold off on the next high tide. The Frenchman said that he had undertaken an extremely difficult and dangerous piece of navigation the night before for the benefit of the Norwegian authorities, and he was not prepared to risk his ship and his ship's company a second time in these treacherous waters in the dark; if, after his efforts, the Norwegians refused to entrust their gold to him, he would refloat his ship and make immediately for the open sea. Before coming to a decision, however, he was prepared to talk to a higher authority.

"Unfortunately there is no higher authority," Johan told him. "I am responsible for the gold reserves."

"You? So young?"

"The Germans gave us no time for careful staff planning," explained Johan, "as I'm sure you know. But with only a few men I have managed to bring it this far."

Time was very short. By high tide, the crew must be back on board to refloat the ship, which meant that they would have to leave in a few minutes' time; the ship's boats would have to be launched again before they could be put to sea.

"Tell me, Captain," said the Frenchman, "do you know anything about the sea?"

"I sail."

The destroyer's Captain smiled. "My position is simply this: I am here, and I am obliged to depart. In my considered opinion, the risks of departing by night are considerably higher than those of departing by day. I will therefore depart by day. That is my decision. Whether I depart with or without my quota of your gold reserves is obviously your decision. Before making up your mind, let me draw your attention to the fact that my ship is especially camouflaged for this trip; we also carry anti-aircraft guns, and my crew know how to use them. Time is short. What do you say?"

Johan made the only decision possible. He accepted the Frenchman's offer.

"I must tell you," the destroyer's Captain said, "that I am in radio contact with the British aircraft-carrier; if necessary, I can request air-cover, although I would prefer not to do so—planes always attract attention. So now you must tell me immediately where your gold is hidden."

"In these lorries."

"But your Sergeant said there was ammunition in the lorries!"

"Did he? We've got into the habit of being ultra-cautious."

"That I understand! . . . I will leave you some men to bring the gold immediately to the nearest quay, while I return with the rest of my crew to the ship to bring her alongside."

Johan walked down with him to where his ship's boats were concealed, watched while they were relaunched and then returned to the tunnel. Meanwhile, his own men and the French sailors got the first of the crates loaded on to the trolleys and began to take them down to the quay.

The French destroyer was refloated without difficulty. By the time she arrived, there were a good number of crates waiting to be loaded. They were busy getting this organized when the French officer of the watch, who was standing on the bridge scanning the sky with a pair of binoculars, called down to the Captain that he could see a plane overhead, flying very high. The only way of making sure whether it was friend or foe was to get in touch with the British aircraft-carrier. She said she had no planes up in that direction, but it might have come from a temporary airfield near Molde; she advised that all activity at the docks should cease immediately while she sent a fighter up to investigate. While waiting, the French sailors got back on board their ship and the Norwegians returned to their tunnel, leaving their precious cargo on the quay.

The German reconnaissance plane had come from Bergen, and was on its way back to base. It was on a routine trip over Molde, and had noticed nothing unusual as it flew over Andalsnes. However, it did notice a British fighter on its way to the port, and wondered why it should have been sent. That it should have come to investigate him did not occur to him; if the British sent up aircraft to investigate every spotter plane they would soon be out of petrol, so he was curious. Putting on his binoculars, he returned for another look, and this time he noticed something at Andalsnes which interested him mightily—small, dark moving shapes. The French sailors, although they had returned to their ship, were still on deck. He headed back to base with all speed to report what he had seen. Bergen got in touch with Trondheim, the nearest German-held airport, and within five minutes a bomber had taken off, heading for the area.

The British fighter had been about to signal an all-clear when he saw the bomber approaching from the north. The enemy plane, flying south, into the sun, did not see the fighter; the British pilot signalled to the destroyer at once: "Enemy bomber approaching from north. Am standing by."

The Norwegians in their tunnel knew nothing of what was going on; their first intimation that something was amiss was the sight of activity on board the French destroyer—the muzzles of the anti-aircraft guns were moving round towards the north. And then they heard the pulsing of the bomber's engines.

"So that's that," said Johan bitterly. "He should have waited until tonight."

The bomber roared overhead. The destroyer's guns went into action, and she sheered off, after dropping two bombs wide of the mark.

The bomber returned to the attack, apparently undamaged, and then, out of the sun, the British fighter swooped down on her like a hawk. The bomber released three more bombs, one of which landed on the bows of the destroyer, one on the quay and one in the water, but, as she climbed again, her rear-gunner was hit by anti-aircraft fire from the destroyer, and in the same instant her pilot was killed by machine-gun fire from the British fighter. The German plane had been flying very low, very sure of herself, and she crashed into the sea before the co-pilot had time to realize what had happened. In spite of an initial warning that a British fighter had been sighted over the area, no one on board the bomber had seen it at all.

As soon as the bomber crashed, the fighter circled low over

the destroyer, flashing the message, "What is your condition?" Receiving the reply, "Stand by", he continued circling, and then shortly afterwards the destroyer signalled again, "Damaged but seaworthy. Sailing to Molde without repeat without cargo for repairs. Please escort." The fighter acknowledged, and then radioed his own message back to base.

The Captain of the destroyer came ashore alone, and started walking slowly and dejectedly towards the tunnel. He saw Johan coming out to meet him, and shrugged eloquently.

"We have lost our forward anti-aircraft gun," he said, "and are practically defenceless. To take the gold now would be to put it too much at risk. As soon as I reach Molde for repairs, I shall request another destroyer to be sent."

"Thank you," replied Johan stonily.

The Frenchman shot him a keen glance. "A ship will come," he said. "Do not despair."

Knut Lerdal, watching a small fire which had been started by the bomb, suddenly realized what it was that was burning. The gold! It was the wooden crates that were burning. . . . He streaked after Johan.

"Sir!" he shouted. "The gold! It'll melt!"

The Frenchman didn't understand what he was saying, but he looked in the direction of the wildly pointing finger.

"Take everyone and throw snow on that blaze," ordered Johan.

Some of the French sailors, watching, immediately ran down to help, and very soon the fire was extinguished. Gingerly they began moving the snow off the crates again, looking for damage; out of one of the partly-burnt crates they noticed a small golden stream on the white background. It had indeed begun to melt, but contact with the snow quickly re-set it.

"Gold," murmured the ship's Captain wonderingly. "Pure gold."

All their hopes had been pinned on that destroyer; it was only as they stood watching it fading from sight that it came home to them that they would have to spend at least another day at Andalsnes—perhaps several—before another destroyer could be found. It was a shattering blow. Johan watched the men piling the crates back on board the lorries in grim silence, and saw Colonel Hagen reappear at the mouth of the tunnel.

All he said was, "Well, that's that! I'll try to get another destroyer to come in tomorrow evening. Tonight's out, I know, and daylight loading is obviously out of the question."

"Sir," begged Johan, "can't we drive to Afarnes tonight and take the ferry to Molde? I'm only a few days ahead of the German army as far as I can see; tomorrow evening might be too late."

"General Ruge's orders are that the lorries are on no account to be ferried across from Afarnes to Molde. More than half the air-cover would have to be diverted to protect them on the crossing, and Molde is now the only port left for the allies to use. . . . But if they can't send a destroyer tomorrow, I'll try to persuade them to let you use the ferry. The pilots will just have to have eyes in the backs of their heads, that's all. Or they could arrange a diversion of some kind while you go across—we'll have to see. And I do agree with you; you can't stay here more than a few days longer."

When he had gone, Johan sat down on a roll of bedding. Carl went over and sat beside him.

"What did Colonel Hagen say?"

"That we should wait. That the ferry was too dangerous. But I can't think of anything worse than just sitting here waiting for the Germans to come and take the stuff in their own good time! Anyhow, if Hagen gets us a ship tomorrow, all might yet be well. . . ."

The day disappeared somehow, and they had already begun to feel quite hopeful that a destroyer would indeed call for the rest of the gold on the following evening.

Their supper was disturbed by the sound of shooting, quite close to them; they listened anxiously, but there was no return fire, but ten minutes later one of the duty-watch came to tell Johan that the Lieutenant of marines who had greeted them on their first evening wanted a word with him. Johan went out at once; he found him with six marines, all looking very nervous and upset.

"Well, Jensen," he said, "what's going on?"

"Some men have been shot," blurted out the younger man, "including Colonel Hagen. He's dead."

"Hagen shot! But by whom?"

"A rifle was fired from the woods, on this side of the

dockyard. I want—that is, the men want—to search this tunnel."

"But—but those woods are outside the dockyard!"

"Yes, sir, I know. But the men are beginning to panic. If you don't agree to an ordinary search under supervision, they're planning to come over and do it themselves."

Johan was alarmed. "Who's your senior officer at the moment?"

"I'm afraid I am. We had two majors until a few days ago, but one was killed in the bombing and the other one's got pneumonia. I'm the senior Lieutenant, sir. I thought if these men were allowed to carry out a search at once, on a friendly basis as it were, just to satisfy themselves that no parachute troops are hidden here——"

With rifles at the ready, the marines searched the tunnel, and after a while returned to Lieutenant Jensen, satisfied.

"Well, as I said, there's no one here except us," said Johan, "but it's obvious that there are still paratroopers about somewhere. Can't you send out a search party?"

"I could," said Jensen, "but I might lose a lot of men. And quite unnecessarily, as the Germans simply can't last much longer. Their food's bound to run out soon, and they've got no water."

"I'm very sorry about Hagen," said Johan, "and his death has left you with a big responsibility. As for us, are you able to arrange about getting us a destroyer from Molde?"

"The Colonel didn't tell me anything about his arrangements for you, I'm afraid," said Jensen. "You'll have to deal with the harbour-master from now on; I think he knows the form. . . . And speaking of water, you're short of it, too, like the rest of us. I'll send a detail with some for you tomorrow morning."

As soon as he had gone, Johan said, "Colonel Hagen was our link with Molde! With him dead, I can't see. . . . Look here, I'm going to see the harbour-master at once, to find out whether Hagen actually sent a message to Molde asking for another destroyer before he was killed. And I'll find out exactly who's down there. If they can't promise me a ship for tomorrow, I'm bloody well going to take matters into my own hands!"

Johan had an extremely frustrating interview with the harbour-master. A destroyer, he was told, had certainly been contacted, and had volunteered to come in and see what it was possible to do. She was coming into Molde on the morning tide, but not until she was there would she give her decision as to whether she would try to come on to Andalsnes or not.

"Call again at about nine o'clock tomorrow morning," said the official. "I should have definite news for you by then."

Johan was just leaving, when he suddenly stopped and turned round again. "If the answer's negative, I'll take the gold to Molde on the ferry whatever they say at the other end. I'm in charge of it, and I won't be messed about any longer. So you can stand by to make that signal tomorrow if necessary—or make it tonight if you like, if there's anyone down there still in authority."

"General Ruge himself is at Molde."

"Oh. . . . Well, then, there *must* be a ship of some sort on the way."

"He may be the Commander-in-Chief, sir, but he's not a magician!"

The harbour-master watched Johan sympathetically as he walked slowly and heavily back to the tunnel. He hadn't the heart to tell him that Molde was in a state of complete chaos, and he would be lucky if even a fishing boat turned up.

Johan returned to his team and told them what the harbour-master had said. "But by God," he added, "if they expect me to wait here much longer while the Germans creep closer I'm bloody well not going to. We'll take the gold up into the Jotenheim Mountains and bury it, and be damned to the lot of them!"

M

SIXTEEN

CONTACT RE-ESTABLISHED

WITH DIFFICULTY Johan waited until nine o'clock the following morning before going to see the harbour-master. Before leaving, he told Carl to keep the duty-watch fully alert during his absence. "I know how you all feel about the marines," he said, "but try to remember what they've been through—yes, them, as well as us. So whenever they call, be courteous."

When he reached the harbour-master's office, one look at the man's face was enough to tell him that something was wrong.

"Molde's off the air, sir, I'm afraid, for the moment," he was told. "There was a heavy raid last night, and they blacked out in the middle of it."

"I see," said Johan. "Any news of the Germans?"

"Plenty of rumours. Nothing definite."

"Something tells me I should leave for Molde tomorrow, orders or no orders."

"No use driving down unless the ferry-boats are expecting you," said the harbour-master patiently. "Can't you see you'd be bombed out of existence, waiting on the quay? The mechanics will probably mend this fault fairly quickly. I'll send a man down to tell you as soon as I'm in contact again."

Johan returned to the tunnel to find the men all in a very bad humour.

"It's the water-ration, sir," explained Carl. "They've cut it, and anyway it's filthy."

"I'm sorry. Can't be much longer now."

But they were destined to spend two more seemingly endless freezing days and nights, short of water, food, fuel and cigarettes, before communications with Molde were re-established.

"Well," asked Johan briskly, as soon as he received the news, "and what orders have you got for me?"

"None, sir, I'm afraid, as yet. But there *is* news, and it's bad news. Terrible news."

"Well, come on, man, out with it!"

"I've just heard that the allies are withdrawing from south Norway."

Johan's heart gave a sickening jolt. "Evacuating? But they *can't* be! They've only just come!"

"They're not calling it an evacuation," said the harbour-master. "It's not as though they were leaving Norway completely. They're going to north Norway, to carry on the fight there."

"But they can't just abandon the greater part of the country, and fight in the Arctic Circle!"

"Sir, they must. With Andalsnes out of action, and Molde under constant attack, our allies and also our own forces are withdrawing to Tromsö. As you know, the road system stops at Bodö—there's no way of getting north except by ship. Unless you ski over the mountains, and plenty of our lads are doing just that. All troops are being pulled back to Molde for shipment north. The place is absolutely packed already, and there'll be more troops coming west tonight. I expect they'll send for you as soon as the place is clear. I shouldn't think you'd find a single tree to hide those lorries under at the moment."

Johan turned away from him. The harbour-master watched him sympathetically. "I sent a signal to General Ruge asking what was to be done about you," he said, "but he's driven up to the Fifth Division. I daren't contact anyone else."

Johan nodded, and left him. And all night long the team lay awake listening to the rumble of vehicles driving through Andalsnes to Vestnes for shipment on the ferries to Molde; the Fifth Division, Norwegians and allies alike, were pulling out.

By first light, Johan had had enough. He trudged purposefully through the snow to the harbour-master's office.

"I want to know whether the *Glasgow*'s come in yet," he said.

"She's expected tonight, at Molde."

"Tonight! Well then, that settles it. Once she's sailed, there'll be nobody left in south Norway to give me any orders if anything happens to Ruge, or if he leaves for the north with everyone else. Is the King still at Afarnes with the Government?"

"As far as I know."

"Then I'd like to get a signal through to Afarnes. Can you do that?"

"I *can*, yes. But we're not allowed to send signals to them, sir. Strict orders."

"I have my own contact at Afarnes." If the Government were still there, Arne would be also; Johan felt that a message to him personally just might get him permission to go to Molde.

The harbour-master would be only too pleased to see the gold on its way, and if the Captain had a contact of his own he would do all he could to see that he got in touch. "Write it down for me and I'll send it off," he said. "And perhaps you'd like to wait for your answer—Afarnes is very small, so there shouldn't be much delay."

Johan took out his pen and wrote, "Permission requested to leave Andalsnes for Molde immediately. Most urgent. Fridtjof." "Please send this to Major Arne Ording," he said.

The official read it through; when he reached the word 'Fridtjof' his eyes widened and he looked up sharply.

"Fridtjof!" he exclaimed. "Do you mean to tell me that you're Fridtjof?"

"It's my code-name. I should have thought Colonel Hagen would have told you. But why——?"

"He did *not* tell me! And let's hope it's not too late now. A message came through for Fridtjof directly we re-established contact with Molde last night. You're to go at once. Here it is; read it for yourself."

Johan snatched the piece of paper from his hand, and read: "Urgent. Instruct Fridtjof to go to Molde soonest and inform me estimated time of arrival at Afarnes. Ruge."

"And another signal for you has just come in," the harbour-master told him. "From Afarnes."

Johan read: "To Fridtjof. Will meet you at Molde today." And it was signed "Magnus."

Johan grinned. "Thank God," was all he could say.

"Well, it was touch and go," said the official. "If you hadn't lost all patience this morning. . . . But I can't be expected to know the Christian name of every man on this dockyard, so I just——"

"You're not to blame," said Johan, "but you must send a signal to Ruge at once before that apparatus of yours blows another fuse. Say, 'Message received proceeding with all possible speed. Fridtjof'. And be sure to give the time, so that he can guess when to expect me, and arrange for the Afarnes ferries to be ready for me."

"Right. And your signal to Major Ording?"

"Send the same to him."

As Johan hastened across to tell his team the good news, he was startled by the sound of sudden shouting, and then the sharp crack of a pistol shot came to his ears; instinctively he threw himself flat on his face. The shot had come from the direction of the tunnel; why the bloody hell hadn't the marines sent out a search-party to round up those remaining parachute troops as he had advised? Now perhaps it was too late. . . . He looked across, measuring the distance between himself and the tunnel. Suddenly more men charged out from the tunnel mouth and set upon the others. He realized then what was happening: in spite of all he had said, his men were attacking the marines.

As Johan ran up, he saw his Sergeant on the ground, cradling young Ringe in his arms; blood was streaming from the boy's shoulder.

"Well, Sergeant," he demanded sharply, "what is the meaning of this?"

The Sergeant got shakily to his feet. "Sir," he said, "the marines brought the water-ration. Carl Ringe was exercising with the men when they arrived, and he went to fetch his cap before getting out of the truck to sign for the water. But, sir, he picked up the wrong cap. . . ."

Johan, following the Sergeant's gaze, looked down; lying on the ground beside Carl was a German officer's cap. He looked into the pain-filled eyes.

"You stupid bastard," he said softly.

"I'm very sorry, sir."

"Is it bad?"

"Luckily the shot only went through my shoulder."

"I'm sorry too, sir," said a Second Lieutenant of marines. "I told him to put his hands up, but he kept coming towards me, grinning. Then your Sergeant yelled at me from the top of one of the trucks, saying something about fancy-dress, and I hesitated, but the gun went off."

"What's up?" It was Per Jensen's voice. While Johan was telling him what had happened, some more men were slowly getting to their feet, and examining three or four more who were still unconscious.

"Please, sir," begged Sergeant Borg, "shouldn't Carl see a doctor as soon as possible?"

"Is there a doctor anywhere about, Jensen?" asked Johan.

"Yes, somewhere. Do you know where he is, Dahl?" he asked, turning to the officer who had shot Carl.

"Yes, sir. I'll fetch him at once. And, sir, I'm terribly sorry——"

"All right. I know. Just fetch the doctor, and be quick about it. . . . It's extremely fortunate your chap wasn't killed," he added, turning to Johan. "Young Dahl's elder brother was murdered the day before you arrived by a German in Norwegian uniform; he was knifed. They've all got the jitters."

"Yes, so I see. . . . Schwartz, chuck out a couple of blankets, will you? We'll have to keep the patient warm till the doctor comes."

Schwartz dived into the front lorry, and reappeared with some German overcoats, which he tucked round Carl. Jensen looked at them wryly. "It's a wonder more of your people aren't shot!" he remarked. "What do you carry all that German gear about for?"

"We've had to use it from time to time on our travels," said Johan vaguely. "Carl, I hope the doctor can patch you up all right. I've just been given the message we've all been waiting for. We're to drive to Molde at once."

"Don't leave me behind!"

"There's no chance of that," announced a new voice; looking round, they saw that Dahl had returned with an army surgeon. "Both hospitals at Andalsnes are flat," he told them, "and I've got too many casualties here as it is, and practically no water. Luckily, I hear you're not too seriously wounded——

just a bullet to extract. By the way, there was an announcement on the radio this morning that would have amused me
if I'd been in the mood for laughing. Germany has declared
war on Norway, as of this morning. Whether the war's official
or unofficial, this place is packed with wounded men. I'm
getting as many of them on to their feet as possible to give
them a chance to get the hell out of here before the enemy
arrives. Get the Lieutenant on to a stretcher."

"Where's Mr Borg?" asked Carl suddenly. They all looked
round, but the Sergeant was nowhere to be seen.

"He's probably gone to take charge of the cargo," said
Johan, although it struck him as odd that he had simply
walked away without waiting for the arrival of the doctor.
"Krefting and Eriksen," he said, "get Mr Ringe on to that
stretcher and stay with him while he's with the doctor. You
others, get back to the tunnel."

On their return, they found Kristian Schwartz in charge.

"Seen Sergeant Borg?" asked Johan.

"He came back, sir, but he didn't look very well. Larsen's
with him."

Johan had a sudden premonition of disaster. Sergeant Borg
was lying on the floor; the men had made a pillow for him,
and covered him with blankets. His face was contorted, and
he was lying quite still.

Olaf Larsen, kneeling beside him, looked up. "Sir, he's been
trying to say something," he said, "but I can't make out what
it is. . . . I'm glad Carl's not too bad; where did the bullet go?"

"Into the shoulder—damned lucky. Unquestionably Borg
saved his life. Let's have a look at him."

Johan knelt down in Olaf's place, but realized at once
that no one would ever know what it was that Rudolf Borg
had been trying to say. "Olaf," he said, "I'm afraid he's
dead."

The duty-watch, who had seen the Sergeant's last walk to
the train, came crowding in. Olaf looked up at them, and
suddenly his face darkened.

"Back to your posts, you lazy sods," he ordered sharply.
"So the Sergeant's dead. So we're all going to miss him. But if
you think discipline has come to an end because he's no longer
with us——!"

He stopped. The truck was empty, except for himself and Captain Olsen.

"A very praiseworthy start, Sergeant Larsen," said the Captain softly. "You are now in charge of your watch; your corporal will be Emil Lerdal. Take Rudolf Borg's stripes, and never forget who they belonged to. . . . If we don't have better luck than this for the rest of the trip," he added bitterly, "you may be a Captain by this evening! You and I began this journey together, Olaf," he said. "Let's try to finish it together."

"Yes, sir. . . . And Carl Ringe?"

"Carl will come with us."

"But, sir, he won't be able to ski for about three weeks— the Germans will capture him!"

"We'll decide what to do on the drive to Afarnes. The Germans will get Ringe over my dead body!"

SEVENTEEN

A CLOSE-RUN THING

IT WAS A GRIM-FACED BODY of men that set out for Afarnes about two hours later. The gold was still intact but their losses were mounting steadily; the one thought in the minds of all was to see their cargo to safety and then return and take their revenge on the Germans.

Olaf Larsen was in the leading lorry with Björnsen, the garage mechanic. Men borrowed from the dockyard drove the next few lorries with the rest of the team behind them, and the rear lorry was driven by Astrup; in the back, in a space specially prepared for it, was Carl Ringe's stretcher. He was still under the anaesthetic, and sitting beside him, waiting for him to wake up, was Johan.

After about half an hour Carl stirred, and then opened his eyes. "Uncle Rudolf?" he asked weakly.

"I'm afraid he's not here; it's me," said Johan. "How are you feeling?"

"Not too bad, sir. Are we on the road to Afarnes?"

"That's right."

He wondered whether to break the news at once to Carl that Rudolf Borg was dead, or wait till they reached Afarnes. The matter was taken out of his hands by Astrup, who had heard them talking.

"Feeling better, Carl?" he called from the cab of the lorry.

"Yes, thanks, Ivor."

"That's good. Old Borg knew you were going to be all right before he died."

"Before he *died*. . . . Uncle Rudolf dead? . . . Sir, who killed him?"

"Nobody killed him, Carl," said Johan gently. "He had a stroke."

Carl's eyes filled with weak tears. "It was my fault."

"Carl, you mustn't blame yourself. He had high blood-pressure—it was written all over him. *Any* shock could have killed him. And he's had one slight stroke already; it happened when the Germans kidnapped him. I saw no point in telling you. . . ."

Johan, desperately tired and anxious, felt unable to cope any longer with the additional burden of Carl's grief. Astrup, his friend, could take over.

The gold lorries were greeted at Afarnes by the harbour-master and two coastguard officials. There was a message from General Ruge, saying that they were to start shipping the gold at four o'clock. The ferries were to be speeded up. It was about five miles to Molde, and the journey normally took about forty-five minutes.

Across the water to the west of them, the team could just make out a pall of smoke; that, the harbour-master told them, was Molde. The town had been burning for days. However, they had managed to keep on the air for most of the time and the bombing had become less frequent, due to the air-cover put up by the British.

After an excellent meal, the team drew apart from their marine drivers, intending to have a sleep while the gold was guarded by dockyard staff, but one by one they started whispering again, anxious and nervous. Their home towns, they realized, would by now all be occupied by German troops and their grand plans for resistance, without weapons, seemed pathetic indeed.

"I don't suppose it'll be all that bad over at Molde," Johan said, in an attempt to cheer them up, "or the King and the Government wouldn't have gone over there this morning."

"It's not that, sir," said Olaf. "We're just wondering what we're going to do after the gold's delivered."

"No need to start worrying about that yet," he said. "The first thing to do is to get the gold over to Molde. We can talk about it then." Johan realized that they feared the time to separate had come, and no one wanted to be the first drivers to go over to Molde, perhaps to be seized and put on a boat and sent up north, never to see his companions again. He decided to send marine drivers across first, with two of his own men as foot-passengers, with orders to contact Major

Ording and find out what the form was, and then come back and report.

Astrup and Krefting were chosen to travel across. After seeing them off, Johan went to talk to Carl; the men had been giving him a lot of pills—Johan only hoped they knew what they were doing. He found him very weak, but calm. "You'll come across to Molde with me, Carl, on the last ferry," he said, "and once there we'll see what's to be done with you."

The second ferry came in from the other side, and two more lorries went off; long before the first ferry was due back, Johan and Olaf were on the quay waiting for it, anxious to hear what Krefting and Astrup had to say.

There was no sign of them on the second ferry, nor on the third. As they stood gazing west, they suddenly realized that what they had taken for a particularly fine sunset was not a sunset at all—it was Molde, in flames.

"You don't think the Germans have taken the port, sir," suggested Olaf nervously, "and are collecting the gold off the lorries as it gets to the other end?"

And then the fourth ferry docked, and Astrup and Krefting leapt off it.

"What the hell have you two been up to?" snapped Johan.

"Terribly sorry, sir!" said Astrup. "You can have no idea what it's like over there—the place is absolutely jam-packed. It was General Ruge who kept us—he wanted to hear all about the journey. They're all so delighted that the gold's safe, and they're all asking for you. The King wants to see you, and he doesn't want the *Glasgow* to sail without you. And he even asked to meet us, and he shook hands with both of us and—and. . . . What else Krefting?"

"Major Ording said to tell you that the English destroyer reached Scotland safely with the first consignment of gold," said Krefting. "They're loading this lot on to the *Glasgow*."

"The *Glasgow*?" exclaimed Johan. "But she's going north! What's the point of that?"

"They say there's a Norwegian ship waiting at Tromsö to take it direct to Scotland," said Astrup. "It's only a hop, they said. The great thing is to get it out of Molde at once."

"Sir, shouldn't you go on the next ferry?" suggested Krefting. "*Glasgow* may sail soon—she'll have to if there's a bad raid. Her skipper's getting nervous; he says he's got the King and the Government on board already, and quite a lot of gold——"

"And the rest?"

"I believe another ship's coming down from Tromsö. . . . But, sir, His Majesty asked me to make sure you didn't miss him. . . ."

Johan paused for a moment, looking round to see who was left. The ninth and tenth lorries were going on this ferry; if he went with them, that would leave only the last two. Olaf Larsen was still at Afarnes, with the last marine drivers; he decided to go now, leaving Olaf and Astrup to bring over the eleventh and twelfth. He himself would take Krefting to drive the other lorry, bringing Carl Ringe.

"Sergeant Larsen," he said, "do you think you and Astrup, with your marines, can bring over the last two lorries, if I go now?"

"Certainly, sir, but how will we know where to go, at the other end?"

"Krefting will meet you."

As Johan's ferry approached Molde he was gradually able to distinguish blazing buildings. The dockyard was still operational.

By the time his ferry docked, it was already dark. He drove ashore at once, and headed straight through the milling crowds towards the centre of the dockyard with Krefting following. As the two lorries switched off their engines, the first thing they heard was a loud-speaker: "This is an air-raid warning! This is an air-raid warning! Those two lorries are to be moved *immediately*. What the bloody hell. . . ?" An incendiary bomb shrieking down put an end to the official's comments, but someone came running towards Johan.

"Move that lorry, boy, quickly. Over here!" It was Arne Ording's voice.

"Arne!" he called, "it's me—Johan!"

"Why, Johan!" exclaimed Arne. "Am I glad to see you! But for God's sake don't commit suicide now you *have* arrived —I'll hop in and guide you to safety."

Johan leaned out of his lorry. "Follow on!" he called to Krefting.

The two lorries were quickly put under cover. The raid did not last very long. British fighters had chased away the enemy.

Arne put his arm through Johan's, and led him away. "*Everyone's* asking for you," he said excitedly. "No one ever thought it could really be done."

They were approaching a crowd of high-ranking officers, Norwegians, British, Polish and French. The gold braid on their full-dress uniforms gleamed in the lurid light of the fires raging all over the stricken port. It was when Johan saw them clustered there, waiting to be taken out to sea, that the full magnitude of the disaster which had befallen his country came home to him with an overwhelming shock. Tomorrow, south Norway would be defenceless, and the Germans would occupy it at their leisure. In that moment, he knew that he at least would not desert his country. His tentative plans to go underground with his team became an irrevocable decision.

Suddenly one of the Norwegian officers noticed him, and in a second he was surrounded by a host of wildly enthusiastic men, all congratulating him and shaking his hand and clapping him on the back. He tried to smile as he acknowledged their congratulations, but his expression remained grim. Arne, noticing, held his arm more tightly. "You're about out on your feet, aren't you?" he said sympathetically, "but you got through. It was a magnificent achievement."

"But you brought out His Majesty and the Government, Arne," Johan answered, carrying on the conversation with difficulty as he acknowledged the endless shower of congratulations with absent-minded handshakes, nods and salutes. "You've done extremely well yourself."

"Actually," Arne admitted, "we've had a fairly easy time of it ever since we took that train at Hjerkinn. We couldn't really understand why it was, until your lads came over here and told us some of your adventures. But now we've been able to work out the reason. Someone at Hjerkinn must have told the Germans that the King was travelling on a train—it was the King they were looking for when the gold-train reached

Dombas station, wasn't it? . . . And I gather they were still on your tail as far as your logging camp at Trollheim, still believing you had him. So you've really done my job as well as your own, haven't you?"

"Well, just so everything worked out all right in the end," said Johan, with a faint smile. "Oh, Arne," he burst out, "did they *have* to desert south Norway quite so soon?"

"Johan, the rescue of the gold means that we will be able to go on fighting back, even after Norway's been occupied. We will be able to buy planes and explosives, train an undercover army. . . ."

Arne suddenly stopped talking, came to attention and saluted smartly. "Sir, here he is," he said. "He's just arrived."

Waiting to greet him with outstretched arms was General Ruge. "Johan!" he exclaimed, grinning broadly. "So you did it! Somehow I knew you would. Your young thugs have been telling me your adventures—what a saga!"

"We had our moments, sir," agreed Johan.

"You certainly did! And I can't tell you how proud we all are, and how grateful. His Majesty went on board during that last raid, but you'll see him on the *Glasgow*."

Johan nodded, without speaking, and then a messenger came up to say that the Prime Minister was asking for the Commander-in-Chief. "I'll see you later, Johan," he said.

"Sir," Johan called after him on a sudden impulse, "could my Lieutenant travel to Tromsö on board the *Glasgow*? I know she's crowded, but he's wounded, and I don't see how we can just leave him for the Germans to pick up."

"Of course."

"Better write out a pass for him at once, sir," put in Arne, "or he'll never get on."

Ruge took out a notebook. "What's his name?" he asked.

"Carl Ringe."

"Ah! The young villain with the private army."

"The same."

"Well, here's a pass for him. I'll look forward to meeting him."

As soon as Ruge had gone on board, Johan, accompanied by Arne, went to fetch Carl from the lorry. He was intensely relieved to see them; he was cold and in pain, and thought he had been forgotten. "If I go to Tromsö, how will I get in touch with the group again?" he asked anxiously.

"When you're better, ski over the mountains and call at my house in Oslo," Johan told him. "You'll get news there. Thanks for all you've done—you'll be showered with congratulations on board the *Glasgow*! I'll look forward to seeing you again soon."

Arne was puzzled by this conversation. As Carl was carried away, he was about to remind Johan that he would see Carl on the *Glasgow*, when a messenger came to say that the cruiser was pulling out in ten minutes. She had 23 tons of gold on board, and a Norwegian merchant ship, the *Driva*, would take the rest to Scotland; the harbour-master would supervise its shipment. And immediately afterwards a wild-eyed, terrified Krefting rushed up to them.

"Sir," he cried, "I've been looking everywhere for you! The ferries—the ferries have been sunk!"

"Sunk? Both of them?"

"Yes, sir, both. What about Astrup and Larsen, and the rest of the gold?"

One look at Johan's face was enough for Arne. "Johan," he exclaimed. "I thought you came across with the last consignment!"

"I came with the second-last; Astrup said the King was asking for me. Two lorries were to follow on the next ferry."

"How much gold?"

"Fourteen tons."

Arne tried to concentrate, and to work out how likely it was that a ferry-boat would have been sunk with the last two lorries actually on board.

"Did you see either of the ferries sunk, boy?" he asked Krefting.

"Yes, yes, I did. Captain Olsen's ferry was sunk within sight of Molde—on its way back to Afarnes. I went at once to tell the harbour-master, and he told me the other one had been sunk too. . . . He got a call from Afarnes, but the lines went dead halfway through the conversation."

"The harbour-master," said Arne, "ought to be able to work out exactly where the other ferry would have been; ferries synchronize."

"I asked him, sir. He said that normally he'd know, but not this evening, because the ferries were told to make the best speed they could. So it might have been anywhere."

"Well," said Arne, forcing himself to speak calmly, "in that case there's a good chance it mightn't even have reached the other side before it was sunk. Five miles is a long way—it could have been anywhere. . . . And if the worst comes to the worst, and the gold's been sunk, we can bring it up again after the war. The water's very deep; the Germans would never find it."

The gold could be brought up after the war, thought Johan; yes, Arne was right about that. But not Astrup. Not little Olaf Larsen. . . . Krefting was still at his elbow, shocked and distressed. "Go at once and tell the others that there's a very good chance the lorries weren't on the ferry," he told him. "I'll get a signal off to Afarnes as soon as it's reconnected. Don't panic."

"They're about to take the *Glasgow*'s gangway up," said Arne. "What the hell are we going to do?"

"You go ahead," said Johan. "I'll attend to this."

"But, Johan, how will you come north?"

Johan gave him a wry smile. "I wasn't coming anyway," he said. "I'm staying in south Norway, with my men. I've got an army of my own, and I intend to use it."

Arne's eyes gleamed. "I had an idea you were up to something!" he said. "A lot of us begged Ruge to let us stay on in the south, but——"

There was a roar from the *Glasgow*: "Are you gentlemen coming on board or not?"

"Arne, you must go," said Johan.

"Yes. . . . If you get news of those missing lorries before we're out of the Molde Fjord, will you send a signal?"

"Of course. And I'll keep in touch anyway—somehow."

Arne ran up the gangway, and Johan stood watching as the *Glasgow* weighed anchor and put quietly out to sea on the tide. Then he turned and walked slowly towards the harbourmaster's office. The team, who had been watching anxiously from a distance, came running over to him.

"Sir, you're staying!" cried Eriksen joyfully. "We weren't sure till the last minute."

"Yes, I'm staying. You didn't really think I'd leave you, did you?"

"You could have had orders."

"Orders hell!"

They grinned. And then Krefting said, "What about Larsen, sir, and Astrup?"

"I'm going to see the harbour-master at once and get him to find out what's happened. And I've also got to arrange to get the rest of the gold shipped."

"Where did you send Carl, sir?" someone wanted to know.

"To hospital at Tromsö. He'll join us in Oslo as soon as he's fit."

Johan found the *Driva*'s master waiting to talk to him; evidently she was one of the vessels that had been carrying troops up north, but had returned for her last trip to find that they had all decided to ski over the mountains instead of waiting for him. "So, if you like, my lads will start loading now," he said. "I'll take the bullion straight to Scotland. There's only one catch; I haven't enough coal to get as far as Scotland, and there's no coal left at Molde."

"Come with me and see the harbour-master," said Johan. "I want to know if he's back in touch with Afarnes yet. Two gold lorries were over there when the ferries were blown up; I must find out whether they're still waiting there, or whether they were sunk with one of the ferry-boats. They were carrying 14 tons of gold—and of course some of my men are missing, too."

"Well, if it turns out that the lorries are still over there stranded, I could sail across there myself and pick up the bullion, and your lads," volunteered the master of the merchant ship.

"Why, of course that's the answer!" agreed Johan thankfully. "The truth is, I'm really too tired to think any more."

The harbour-master told them that Afarnes was still off the air; he would keep trying. In the meantime, they concentrated on the problem of coaling the *Driva*. The harbour-master suggested loading up and then calling at Kristiansund for coal before crossing, but this, to Johan's relief, the ship's master firmly refused to do. Kristiansund, he said, was in flames. The harbour-master decided to make a signal to

N

Gjemnes. Here he had better luck. "They've got a coaling
ship already loaded up there," he said. "They were standing
by in case they were needed for the evacuation. They've
promised to send her down at once. I'll let you know as soon
as she's signalled."

The *Driva*'s master went off to supervise the loading of
the bullion left lying on the quay. Johan returned with the
harbour-master to his office, and started to pace up and down.

"You don't need to wait here, sir," said the official. "You
go and get some rest. I'll tell you if I get any news."

"I would prefer to stay," said Johan, "and I want you to
try Afarnes every ten minutes. I must know as soon as possible
what's happened to my men, and the gold."

Left behind at Afarnes, Olaf Larsen took the others inside for
a drink, but he kept glancing nervously at his watch, and,
long before time, they were all standing in the snow looking
out to sea watching for the incoming ferry. As they gazed
across the water which separated them from their friends,
the glowing red blur which had been Molde changed suddenly
into a dramatic firework display. The port was under heavy
air attack. With relief they realized that the raid had only
been a short one, but a few minutes later they heard a droning
sound, growing rapidly louder. A lone bomber was coming
straight towards them; they could tell from its engines that
it was in trouble, and was presumably escaping from the fight.
As it passed low over Afarnes, it dropped its last bombs with
appalling effect: one sank the empty ferry which was just
returning, and the other scored a direct hit on one of the gold
lorries. The boys had all thrown themselves flat on their faces
as the bomber dived, and when they heard it crash eventually
somewhere beyond them, they got shakily to their feet to go
and assess the damage.

"Olaf, what on earth are we going to do?" cried Astrup in
dismay.

"We'll just have to rely on the other ferry," said Olaf, "and
while we're waiting for it, we'd better collect the crates from
that smashed lorry, and also all the gold bars from the split
crates. I expect we can get some help and just throw it on to
the ferry—there'll be plenty of people to unload at the other

end. We'd better get the harbour-master to send a signal to Molde, or they'll wonder why we aren't coming over."

As he spoke, they saw a coastguard official coming slowly towards them. "Well," he said, "you got most of it over. What will you lads do now?"

"Wait for the other ferry, of course," snapped Olaf. "What else would you expect us to do?"

"The other ferry? The other ferry's been sunk, too. On the Molde side." He looked at the men's ashen faces with sympathy. "Come on, lads," he said, "come and have a drink. No one can say you didn't do your best."

"I don't give a damn what anyone can say!" shouted Olaf savagely. "I want another lorry, some petrol, and as many men as you can get hold of."

The man looked at him in astonishment. "What do you plan to do, lad?"

"I'm taking the rest of the bullion to Vestnes. We can get a ferry to Molde from there."

"It's a terribly long drive."

"Longer by road, shorter by sea," replied Olaf briefly. "Anyway, the longer it is, the sooner we'd better get started. I want a lorry here in five minutes flat, and men immediately...."

Astrup grinned in spite of himself; Larsen might have been a Sergeant for years! They asked if a signal could be sent to Molde, but were told this was impossible—the plane had brought down the lines when it crashed. "Well, let's start in to work," suggested Astrup. "It'll keep us warm."

The wreckage was scattered over quite a wide area. With their pocket torches they went about collecting gold bars from split crates and putting them into piles, helped by their two remaining marine drivers. Reinforcements and a lorry arrived with surprising speed. At last they were off.

If they could keep up this pace, they might yet be in time to catch the *Glasgow*. They were frightened that Captain Olsen would be ordered to sail in her, and there would be no one to report to at Molde. Ten minutes after they had left, Olaf's co-driver gave a shout. "Sergeant Larsen, they're bombing Afarnes—it's burning!"

Olaf grunted; if he hadn't chased up those lousy sods, they'd be burning, too.

They sped back through the dead town of Andalsnes, and from there they struck the better road to Vestnes. They reached Vestnes at ten o'clock, and hooted their horns wildly. An anxious coastguard official appeared; he was a bit scared of the frantic, dishevelled youth who demanded instant passage to Molde at such an hour and on such a night, and would not believe the lorries were carrying gold until Olaf opened one up and showed him. Convinced, he got things moving at once; there was a ferry moored on the Vestnes side, and its crew were brought from their homes and ordered to take her to Molde immediately. To Olaf's vast relief, the Vestnes ferry was large enough to take both lorries. As soon as they were safely aboard, and could hear the engines of the ferry-boat starting to chug, all four young men fell asleep.

As Johan waited on with the harbour-master at Molde in the faint hope that a signal might be received from Afarnes, he heard someone running up the stairs. He turned round, and there, framed in the doorway, filthy but still recognizable, stood Olaf Larsen.

"Olaf, my dear boy. . . !"

He was across the room in an instant, and had seized Olaf in a bear-like hug. "How on earth did you get across? Did you swim?"

"No, sir, we came from Vestnes, lorries and all. One lorry was a write-off, so we had to borrow another, and transfer the cargo, or we would have been here sooner. When I saw we'd missed the *Glasgow* I was terribly upset—I thought you'd sailed in her."

"I—I still can't believe you're really here!" said Johan. "I'd given up hope. . . . And you're all here, you say. And the gold as well?"

"Yes, sir. We're all here. And all the gold—give or take a bar or two."

"Congratulations," said the harbour-master. "An absolutely splendid effort! . . . I'll arrange for *Driva*'s master to take the bullion, sir—she's still coaling—but in the meantime, hadn't you better get off a signal to *Glasgow*? She'll soon be out of visual range."

"Yes. Yes, of course. Please send to *Glasgow* : ' "Fridtjof" to

"Magnus". Mission completed. All well. Keep in touch. Good-bye.' "

The message was being flashed as he dictated it, and they both looked anxiously out to sea.

"Do you think she saw it?"

"She's answering; here it comes. ' "Magnus" to "Fridtjof",' he read. " 'Warmest congratulations. Communicate soonest. Good-bye and good luck."

As the light stopped flashing, Johan was conscious of an inexpressible weariness, and also a great loneliness. He picked up the sleeping form of Olaf Larsen, and walked heavily downstairs. Tomorrow, in borrowed civilian clothes, they would ski into the mountains.

APPENDIX I

Extracts in Translation of the Speech of General Otto Ruge, Commander-in-Chief of the Norwegian Army, broadcast from North Norway before the Surrender in June, 1940.

When the German invasion took place, the sea defences—ships and coastal batteries—were mobilized and had been mobilized since September, except that unfortunately the mines had not been laid. In the case of the land defences, the situation was quite different. Apart from a few battalions, functioning as neutrality guard, the Army was not mobilized.

It was not until Tuesday morning, when the Navy and the coastal forts were already fighting, that the order was issued for mobilization of the Army. This order did not even reach all divisions. The only intimation of mobilization which reached the country was a radio speech by the Defence Minister to the effect that mobilization was going on. And this was denied soon afterwards by the Oslo Radio, which had in the meantime been seized by the Germans.

While this went on the Germans had taken all the arsenals in southern Norway and many of the mobilization centres and most of the supplies. They had occupied the broadcasting stations and broken off all important telephone and telegraph connections. The Supreme Command, the commanders of the five southern divisions (Norway had only six divisions, one being in the north), as well as a number of regimental staffs, had been obliged to leave their quarters. And their mobilization files were in the hands of the Germans.

What happened during the first forty-eight hours is not very clear. Every officer had to act on his own judgment, based on what he knew, or, more often, did not know, about the situation. Groups of individuals, who were not already in the hands of the Germans, tried to get together, fighting as they went along. As early as Tuesday morning, small isolated groups were fighting round about the country.

When I took over command (April 10th), what was known at

General Headquarters was only this: Around Oslo from Eidsvold in the east to Solihögda in the west, dispersed Norwegian units were trying to break the German onslaught. At Elverum detachments of the Österdal regiment were gathering. It was not clear whether or not we had any forces in the Glomma Valley and around Kongsvinger. It was believed that there must be some Norwegian troops in Östfold, but we did not know and it was impossible to find out. Nothing was known of conditions in Telemark, in the Kristiansund area, at Stavanger, or in the Trondheim area. But we knew that the Bergen Division had tried to mobilize at Voss and the Möre Regiment at Romsdal.

After the lapse of a week, we were informed in a circuitous way by officers we had sent out that isolated detachments of the First Division were at Mysen, of the Third Division at Setesdal, east of Stavanger, and of the Fifth Division at Stören and around Steinkjaer. But we were at a loss as to the numbers of these forces and the amount of arms and ammunition at their disposal.

When General Headquarters did not know more, you will understand that the individual local commanders knew even less. The Oslo Radio worked systematically to increase the confusion; instructions from our own Government did not get across the country.

In the north of Norway, the situation was far more hopeful. The German force at Narvik was isolated. The Sixth Division was already to a large extent under a determined commander, General Carl Fleischer. But we had no opportunity to render assistance from southern Norway. General Fleischer had to look after himself.

What we had to do was to keep a firm foothold somewhere in southern Norway, preferably in Tröndelag, where it seemed that the Allies could most easily land. Allied help was promised on a large scale, and at once. It was our task to keep going, and protect Tröndelag from the south. With the weak and improvized forces at our disposal, practically without artillery, it was impossible for us to engage in any decisive battle before the Allies came to our aid. All we could do was to hold a position till the Germans became too strong for us, then fall back quickly some distance and repeat the same game there. In this way we fought our way back through eastern Norway from one position to another to Dovre, gradually drawing eastwards what we could of our forces at Voss and Romsdal. It was a constant race against time, on the one side the Germans pressing ever harder, on the other the anxiously awaited Allies.

At last the Allies began to come, and in such numbers that I felt sure the crisis would soon be past. Then came the decision of the Allies to retire from southern Norway and Tröndelag. The decision was made after deliberations which I cannot discuss now, but for us Norwegians it was a hard blow. Our troops were exhausted, our supplies depleted. Left alone against increasing German pressure, we could do nothing.

Remember what kind of an army this was. From Oslo, for instance, came hundreds of men who could not mobilize because the Germans held Oslo. They gathered round some leader and became a 'company'; they met other groups of the same kind and became a 'battalion', under the command of some officer. Casually assembled infantrymen, artillerymen, sailors and aviators, with cars and chauffeurs collected from God knows where, became fighting units.

The railway station at Dombas was bombed every day, and the railway and telephone communications broken, but every night it was repaired sufficiently for use.

I bring to mind my 'travelling' officers, who were sent wherever the need was greatest—always in the firing line.

And I say to myself: I admit that many things might have been better, that some persons from whom we might have expected more failed us, and that others did not seem to know there was a war on. Nevertheless in those weeks my faith in my people grew; I have seen their willingness to sacrifice, their endurance, their confidence and their courage. This people will not die.

APPENDIX II

Extracts from the Memorandum delivered to the Royal Norwegian Government from the German Government by the German Minister, Doctor Bräuer, on the night of April 8th–9th, 1940, followed by a list of their orders for co-operation.

Contrary to the sincere wish of the German people and of their Government to live in peace and friendship with the English and French peoples, and despite the lack of any reasonable ground for a conflict between them, the rulers in London and Paris declared war on the German people.

With the outbreak of this war of aggression against the existence of the German Reich and the German people, for which they had long been preparing, England and France began a sea war which was aimed also against the neutral world.

By attempting, in complete disregard of the most elementary rules of international law, to establish a hunger blockade against German women, children and old people, they at the same time subjected neutral states to their ruthless blockade measures. In addition, this English method of proceeding dealt a destructive blow to the conception of neutrality itself.

Germany, for her part, made every effort to safeguard the rights of neutrals. But the German Government possesses documentary proof that England and France have jointly decided, if necessary, to carry out their actions through the territory of the Northern States, against the will of the latter.

Germany is not prepared to tolerate, or inactively to await, such a realization of the plans of her opponents. The German Government has therefore to-day begun certain military operations which will result in the occupation of strategically important points in Norwegian territory. The German Government therefore takes over the protection of the Kingdom of Norway during this war. Germany is resolved, from now onwards, with all the forces at her disposal, to defend peace in Norway against any Anglo-French attack, and to safeguard it definitely.

It is therefore in no hostile spirit that German troops enter

Norwegian territory. The German Government are convinced that by taking this action they are at the same time serving the interests of Norway.

The German Government therefore expects the Royal Norwegian Government and people will regard the German action with comprehension, and will offer no resistance to it. *Any resistance would have to be, and would be, broken by the German occupying forces with all the means at their command, and would therefore result only in entirely useless bloodshed.* The Royal Norwegian Government is therefore requested to take all measures as rapidly as possible to ensure that the action of the German troops may proceed without friction or difficulty.

The German Government requests the Royal Norwegian Government to take the following measures immediately:

1. The Government should issue an appeal to the people and army to refrain from all resistance to the German troops when they occupy the country.

2. It should order the Norwegian Army to enter into liaison with the German troops entering the country, and conclude the necessary agreements as to loyal co-operation with the German command. The Norwegian troops should be allowed to retain their arms insofar as their behaviour should permit. As a sign of their willingness to co-operate, a white flag of truce should be hoisted alongside the national flag on all military buildings approached by the German forces. Liaison detachments should be sent, a) to the Commander of German troops entering the Capital, (military, naval and air officers), and b) to the local troop-leaders. The German Commander shall reciprocally send liaison officers to the Norwegian High Command. The object of the liaison should be to secure a frictionless co-operation and prevent clashes between German and Norwegian troops.

3. The military appliances and buildings needed by the German forces to secure Norway against an external enemy, especially the coastal fortresses, should be handed over undamaged.

4. Detailed information in writing should be placed at the disposal of the Germans regarding any mines which might have been laid by the Norwegian Government.

5. A complete black-out of Norwegian territory for aerial defence purposes should be carried out from the evening after the first day of occupation.

6. The maintainance of means and ways of communication and

of information should be kept up and safeguarded without damage to them. The means of communication (the railway), the internal and coastal shipping and the centres of information should be placed at the disposal of the German forces of occupation to the extent necessary for their work and subsistence.

7. War and merchant ships should be forbidden to leave the country, and no plane should be allowed to take off.

8. Norwegian pilots should be instructed to continue their services according to the requirements of the German authorities, and lighting along the Norwegian coast should be directed on instruction from the German authorities.

9. The service of weather reports should be kept up and put at the disposal of the German army of occupation, but public weather reports should cease.

10. The carriage of all news and mail over sea to foreign countries should be stopped. News and postal connections with the Baltic states should be confined and supervized.

11. The Press and Radio should be charged only to publish military news with the approval of the German Army authorities, and all broadcasting stations should be placed at the disposal of the German command for their announcements.

12. An export prohibition should be prepared against the conveyance of war material from Norway to foreign countries.

13. The repetition of all proclamations and orders which would be issued in accordance with the above points should in the first place, insofar as wireless was used, only be made in a cipher or code not known to Germany's enemies. The commander of the forces of occupation should decide if messages in clear from broadcasting stations could be permitted.

INDEX